Estranged

HEALING FROM TRAUMA AND THE WORLD'S WORST BREAKUP

Estranged

HEALING FROM TRAUMA AND THE WORLD'S WORST BREAKUP

BELLA RAGAZZA

Contents

Dedication: vii

A Note to My Readers ix

Disclaimer

Foreword xi

Preface xvii

Chapter 1: Water Trickles Down 1

Chapter 2: Purpose in the Pain 9

Chapter 3: Bad Blueprints 19

Chapter 4: One Tough Mother 25

Chapter 5: Daddy's Girl 32

Chapter 6: Broken Heart 37

Chapter 7: Now You See Me, Now You Don't 46

Chapter 8: Cool Comfort 53

Chapter 9: Spilt Milk 60

Chapter 10: Where There is One 63

Chapter 11: Order in the Court 67

Chapter 12: Cold Calling 70

Chapter 13: Sweet Sensations 73

Chapter 14: The Breaking Point 78

Chapter 15: They Love Me, They Love Me Not 85

Chapter 16: The World's Worst Breakup 91

Chapter 17: Facing Triggers 99

Chapter 18: Here Comes the Judgment 107

Chapter 19: Freedom Awaits—The Child 111

Chapter 20: Freedom Awaits—The Parent 116

Chapter 21: Conversations 123

Chapter 22: Sneaky Truths 129

Chapter 23: Stayin' Alive—What's in Your Toolkit? 138

Chapter 24: A Final Word on Self-Love and Authenticity 155

Afterword 159

My Love Letters 168

A Poem for You: The Knowing 174

Resources 176

Dedication

To my daughter, my first true love, and my son, the beacon of hope for all the world to see. I love you both so much more than my actions often demonstrated, and my love is eternal.

I am grateful for all you have shown me, proud of all you have become, and humbled by the process of loving you both and losing one of you.

Thank you for believing in me when you did, and in some instances, as you still may do. Most of all, thank you for driving me to the depths of my soul to free me from myself.

The world is a better place because each of you plays a beautiful part in its creation.

To my mother, who played a massive role in shaping who I am today. Although our story seems negative at first, a more in-depth look reveals that the pressure, struggles, and grief we both endured made us stronger and more resilient. I am devoted to carrying on that legacy of growth, strength, and resilience. Our shared tumult and pain drive me to speak up, and out, on the issues we both faced, so that others can become aware and get the support they need. *Water does indeed trickle down. I love you.*

To my father, who remains my hero. I know so little about you, but I like our story just the way it is. I am forever grateful to you, and love and miss you to this day. "Chin up, buttercup." I'm on it, Dad.

To my brothers, each of whom played such pivotal roles in my life growing up. I can say from my now-healed heart that I love you all.

In memory of my niece, who showed me what Grace and reconciliation looked like. You changed my heart forever.

To my love, who has stayed beside me during the ups and downs of figuring this out. May there be better days ahead for us both. Thank you for your support.

To my extended family and friends. Thank you all for the part you have played in my journey. I know it wasn't always easy to be with me.

To the therapists and coaches who helped me through my darkest days, encouraging me to keep writing and working on myself. Some old, some new, and *all* wonderful—thank you.

To the beautiful souls who took the time to share their stories with me and participated in the healing that can only come from acknowledging the darkest parts of ourselves. It was an honor to get to know each of you. I am grateful for your feedback, and for some of the most heartfelt hugs I have had in years. You are all greatly appreciated.

Last, but certainly not least, to my Lord and Savior, Jesus Christ—who takes me as I am, uses me when He can, and loves me despite my rebellious ways. Please keep my heart contrite, and my soul readied for Your work. I love you.

Every person who has been a part of my life is so special.

I once read that life is like a bus. There will be people who get on, some who get off, and some who remain seated for the entire ride. We don't know who will stay, who will go, or the length of the trip they signed up for.

Thank you ALL for being a part of my journey.

Eternal gratitude, love, and light, Bella

A Note To My Readers

There are references to several true stories in this book. All names and circumstances have been altered to protect the parties' privacy.

Disclaimer

In no way does this book purport to provide medical advice.

If you have suicidal thoughts, call 911 immediately.

This is not a treatment program, nor is it designed to take the place of professional advice, therapy, medications, or support.

I share my story, and the stories and input of others I have met along my journey, for informational purposes only.

Foreword

When I was 26 years old, I decided to cut my parents out of my life. I had wrestled with the idea for years, going back and forth, particularly with the relationship with my mother. I kept coming back to that "maybe it will be different this time" moment. Sadly, though, things never changed. I eventually made the hard decision to cut her and my father both out of my life for good.

What unfolded in my reality after making this challenging choice was nothing short of miraculous. For the first time in my life, I could speak my mind freely without fear of judgment. I started releasing videos on my LinkedIn, and within just a few months had a following of people eager to hear from me, people who accepted me, who respected me, and—most of all—who allowed me to feel good about being my true self, just as I am. My parents couldn't provide this for me, and I didn't find an avenue to provide it for myself until I had removed them, and their childish, manipulative nature, from my life altogether.

Something strange kept happening; my life just kept getting better. Contrary to the popular belief that family is everything, in my case, family had to become nothing. Within two months of posting videos consistently on my LinkedIn, I had generated over six figures in revenue for the marketing company I was managing at the time. Without my family in the picture, I flourished and thrived. More importantly, I developed the self-confidence and self-love to finally leave that job and start my own agency. Within months of that move, I had grown tens of thousands of followers, made incredible business and personal connections, broken up with my toxic (now ex) boyfriend, launched and scaled my own marketing agency, and by the time I was 27 years old, I was a self-made millionaire.

But my parents? They were gone.

As much as it saddened me to not have my parents in my life, I finally accepted the consequences of living the life of my dreams and achieving my highest potential. Some children are blessed with the gift of self-reflective parents who genuinely want to work on themselves for the benefit of not only themselves but their kids. These were not my parents. Over time, it became apparent that my success, achievement, and personal fulfillment only grew because I had rid myself of the toxicity of my family dynamic. And yes, even the very souls who gave us life can be too toxic to stick around as we grow older and begin to live a life on our own terms.

It has been over two years now since I've spoken to my parents, and I pray for them and send them love often. I don't know what the future holds for our relationship or if we'll ever rekindle things or find harmony in our relationship where we all feel respected, cared for, and loved. What I do know is this: When I started speaking openly about my parents and my estrangement from them on my LinkedIn blog, I was met with lots of harsh criticism from—you guessed it—parents themselves.

While I did find support through my blog, I also found a lot of doubt: people shamed me for "disrespecting" my parents, called me a brat, said no excuse in the world could justify not talking to one's parents. Still, I stood my ground and maintained my truth that, yes, my life only got better after I removed them from it. I'm not happy about it, but it's simply the reality.

No doubt I've triggered several parents on LinkedIn who perhaps themselves manifested an adult child who no longer speaks to them. Those parents are often struggling to take ownership, responsibility, and—God forbid—look in the mirror for a second to consider how they are, in fact, the creator of this outcome. This is the demonic nature of narcissistic parenting regardless of its root cause.

But one day, I received a message from a parent that was very different from the rest. I will never forget it. It stood out like a sore thumb. This woman in my LinkedIn inbox reached out to me, *thanking* me for my content on narcissistic parenting and dysfunctional families, stating that after a ton of inner-work, she could now see how she was, in fact, the cause of her adult daughter no longer speaking to her, and while in pain, she finally understood why her child needed to make that choice.

WOW! You mean to tell me it is possible? Are there really parents out there taking responsibility for their children's estrangement and not simply playing the victim? This message told me there was at least one. Of course, the message caught my eye right away, and the woman and I began to engage.

I could tell she felt so much fear in speaking out, as we're often taught in society to shield ourselves from shame at all costs. Yet, this woman was laying her shame all out there. I sensed she was even afraid of what I may think of her due to the situation with my own parents. I believe I surprised her when I said, "This message means more to me than you'll ever know. To know there are parents out there like you, who can admit fault, who do see their part in it, and who are willing to change, is all I need to know exists. This message and your bravery keep me moving forward on those days that I feel absolutely hopeless about the epidemic of narcissistic parenting."

That woman, while likely sharing some dark similarities with my own parents, couldn't see she was also my hero. She did the very thing I'd hoped and prayed my parents would do for years: she changed.

Life is about forgiveness. Second chances. Patience, understanding, and rigorous honesty we often love to avoid. Thank you, to this mother, for standing up for what's right and for being willing to face criticism, judgment, shame, and so much more. I honor you and any parent like you who has the courage to stand up for what's right and own up to their past mistakes.

This mother may feel alone now, but I know she's just paving the way for more parents to start having this conversation. She's human, she's flawed, she's made mistakes parenting, and now she's come out of the dark to be a beacon of light for parents everywhere, finally willing to get brave and heal.

Today, this woman I speak of is not only my good friend, she's the author of this groundbreaking book you hold in your hands. Although she writes under a pen name to protect her family, I assure you she is the real deal.

This is "Bella Ragazza," and this is her incredible story.

~ Shay Rowbottom – April 2021
CEO Shay Rowbottom Marketing
CEO Shay Rowbottom Healing—"The Heal Tribe"

Dear Reader:

I found Shay while searching for answers in places where estranged adult children speak up about their experiences—group therapy, private social media groups, blogs, podcasts—in the underbelly of the beast. At first, I felt like I hated her. The pain was intense as I listened to her podcast, read her blog, and watched her thrive in the absence of her parents.

I admitted that to her on a "Heal Tribe" call and she asked me "why did you keep listening to me?" I answered, "because I wanted to understand life through my daughter's eyes, and you were the closest thing I could find. So, I kept leaning in."

Eventually, as I accepted the reality that I had created, Shay's messages landed in a way that moved me from anger and victimhood to compassion for her and the many kids who suffered from the varying degrees and reasons why their home was hell. She helped me to understand what I needed to learn so I could share my story with you. May it help you as much as Shay has helped me with her truth and now her healing group.

Thank you, Shay, for accepting me and for helping me to find a better path.

Love and gratitude,

~BR

PREFACE

I have written this book under the pen name Bella Ragazza, Italian for "beautiful girl," which is how I want my daughter to see herself, and how I wish I had felt growing up.

The front cover illustration for this book depicts my face as an iceberg where my frozen tears had finally begun to flow. They wouldn't stop, and I floated, almost submerged, but not quite. I tasted the salt as I existed in a state of suspended animation, unsure of rising or sinking into what seemed an insurmountable level of grief to push through.

My wake-up call and most profound meltdown that finally thawed the tip of this iceberg began after more than a year of no contact from my adult daughter. Several years before that had passed with scant or perfunctory communication at best. Once the reality of the separation hit me, I began to accept that my "new normal" did not include her.

Reaching this realization involved a process that took me face-to-face with my greatest adversary—*myself.* I resorted to the only thing I knew to do when in such great pain: write. This is my story of estrangement from my daughter—past, present, and future.

Before I was even sure of my intent, I began scribbling this mix of confession and journal, hoping to find a better way to recognize and heal the trauma of my past while forgiving myself for passing it on to yet another generation.

I have worked long and hard to get to the point where I can speak publicly about estrangement and mental health despite my former feelings of shame and fear of judgment. It's still a bit scary to dip my toes into the waters of this uncomfortable conversation, but I'm doing it here, with this book, because I know so many who share this kind of experience and I want to be able to help and support others on this journey. At times I have felt like I was truly dying from a broken heart. If you have felt this way, too, I want you to know you are not alone.

When I first started writing, I wanted a way to share my story in a meaning-ful, upbeat way, but putting a positive spin on the narrative never felt right to me. Instead, page after page seemed to scream with pain and sorrow. I needed to face that reality. In the end, I offer you here my unvarnished truth. I share some of the strategies and thought processes that helped me to accept my situation, work on self-love, and find the inner-peace I so desperately craved. I've done more harm than good at times in my life, and in the process, I lost one of the most precious things to me: my daughter. If I can help just one other parent to avoid losing their child, all this pain will have been worth it. We often deal with a lack of empathy from others, especially those who have lost children to physical death. The belief that children "drift and then grow up and come around" is prevalent. Such mes-sages can serve to diminish your loss, and add to the layers of confusion you deal with as you feel unable to share and be received in a loving way. Hopefully, this book will validate that your feelings are real and legitimate, but also give you some structure on how to move forward despite the situation.

In this world, so much content speaks to resonating with your "best self." Are you sitting out there, like me, looking at all the social media posts, videos, podcasts, and books and thinking to yourself, "What the hell are these people talking about? I'm just trying to survive." Raise your hands, all of you out there who are just trying to survive. Because you know what? I get it.

But surviving isn't thriving, and you may think you'll never thrive again. So, I invite you to reconsider how you define "thriving" for right now.

The shelves are stocked with books about rising up, leaning in, pushing through, creating, and crushing life. Precious few books offer strategies for avoiding selling out and living a life detrimental to those around you or learning to understand *why* we get caught in reactive traps triggered by untreated trauma and mental illness. I'm sharing my story with you as a way of showing you that you can get to the truth of your own story. You can learn how to face that truth. The solemn promises that were broken, moments of despair, and the excuses we use to substantiate our choices. As I did, you can learn how to change your responses, to make healthy decisions to repair and nurture your relationships. This book is a place where the wounded meet the wounded, not to reconcile, judge, or criticize, but to understand, accept, and *let go.*

In this narrative, you'll see that I weave together the story of my past with the lessons I finally learned in the present. I hope to inspire you to think about *your* history and story in much the same way. Think about the choices you made, the outcomes of those choices, the forgiveness you need, and the new lens you can use to view your entire life's landscape. Sadness resides in these pages, but so does hope. Self-love and healing in our lives *is* possible, with or without specific people. If you remain open-minded as you examine my old narrative and your current one, I hope you discover similarities and truths that will help you to find healing in your own life.

As I examined my history, patterns emerged, allowing me to address each underlying event one by one. I learned the value of building energetic bridges rather than raising energetic walls. Each day I lean into taking accountability for my own actions and do my best to improve on where I was the day before. I've learned to own the phrase, "I'm sorry; you deserved better." I've learned to let go of *my* version of an ideal outcome, and instead, focus on what serves the highest good of all: peace.

I am not a psychologist, teacher, guru, influencer, coach, or successful CEO. I haven't hit significant career milestones, hosted a successful podcast, or even consider myself a "qualified" person regarding mental health. You may ask yourself, "Then, why should I read your book?" Because I am an average, ordinary human who has kicked her own ass with self-sabotage, poor choices, misdiagnosis, and the law of sowing and reaping. I am still standing, just like you, and I am still working every day to thrive despite the grief, so I can remain standing.

The concept of family estrangement can be challenging and painful for parents who perceive it to be a sudden event. In reality, it was likely a choice the child was weighing for some time. In the cases of the adult children I spoke to, breaking ties from their family was something they had considered for *years* before actually doing it. Some well-known public figures have made headline news by speaking out on this subject, and about their childhood experiences and their pain. For the parents, societal shame continues, and the myth of divine motherhood prevails. The phrase, "She's your mother; how can you do this to her?" comes to mind.

I am a part of numerous large Facebook groups comprising mostly mothers of adult estranged children, and the common, achingly painful theme in these groups is "Why is this happening? I was a good mother." While this may be true through their eyes, *something* caused the child to decide to stop having contact with them. The abrupt shock the parent experiences from being cut off is diametrically opposed to the years of accumulated pain, trauma, and defeat on the child's part. With each person feeling their viewpoint is the right one, this leaves little room to see things from the other's perspective. In the absence of this understanding, we get defensive. It doesn't help that the current culture still supports the "Honor Thy Father and Mother" commandment and rhetoric at the expense of the child's well-being.

Dr. Richard P. Conti conducted a study of 354 undergraduate and graduate students, noting that 154 participants (43.5 percent) reported experiencing estrangement from one or both parents, with 26.6 percent reporting extended estrangement.[i] He went on to conclude that estrangement "is perhaps as common as divorce in certain segments of society." Another study conducted in Great Britain by Dr. Lucy Blake at the Centre for Family Research at the University of Cambridge, concluded that out of 807 participants, over 450 were estranged from their mothers.[ii]

Estrangement is not an uncommon occurrence.

So why aren't we talking about it? With both the parents and the adult children experiencing conflicting messaging, pressure, and guilt, neither parties do much talking except within the echo chambers of private groups or therapy sessions where *their* choices and viewpoints are accepted. While this may help each individual to feel validated, it does little to solve the crisis or prevent it from happening in the first place. In some instances, families hand down generations of untreated mental illness, trauma, and unresolved issues, and they often lack the communication skills and self-awareness needed to see their situation through a clear lens. Hopefully, this book will provide some clarity and help you shift the way you view your current landscape.

Rather than trying to identify all the possible explanations as to why things are the way they are, this book aims to emphasize the importance of simply owning the problem, finding a way to stop the harm, and trying to repair the damage. Past a certain point, the cause, the why, doesn't matter anymore. All that matters is interrupting the abusive behaviors and learning new ways to live and function.

I have come to consider my life as a tapestry with the rough side showing. It's messy and knotted in some spots, but I'm finding that it can all come together gradually as a uniquely beautiful and valuable portrayal, despite what my past or current circumstance may seem to dictate. I invite you to share this journey with me. Perhaps getting this mayhem of a life off my chest, will also help you to see that something in your own life may need attention. The pain is real. The problem is epidemic. We are asleep behind the wheel and need to wake up. This is me, sounding the alarm.

CHAPTER 1

Water Trickles Down

My daughter was just over seventeen when she took the first step of breaking ties. We had been fighting for years, and she was a senior in high school. Knee-deep in the college process with her father, our fighting escalated as the subject of college loans and my inability to pay for them came up. On one of many hysteria-filled calls, I screamed at her, filled with rage. I believed that she felt entitled to attend an expensive school with no concern for how I could afford my share of the loans and didn't realize she was in the car with her dad and had the phone on speaker. Having heard the way I was behaving towards her, her father decided she should live with him.

I didn't realize this plan was put into place nor did I expect the move, but I came home from work one night to find her entire room cleaned out. I don't know why it shocked me or how I managed to feel sorry for *myself* instead of her, but I did. In retrospect, she must have been planning that move and escape from my unrelenting, moody behavior since she was a child. Although we still kept in touch, things were never the same from that point on. I wasn't a meaningful part of her life while she was in college, and she stayed away for many years post-graduation.

As captives must fantasize about the day when they will again feel sunlight on their faces, so must a child fantasize about the day when they are no longer reliant upon people and situations that keep them feeling insecure, and not validated or safe. Our children's actions may appear spontaneous, but they are far from it. What springs up suddenly is the moment of courage the day they find a solution to their problem. In my daughter's case, she turned 17 and was willing to drive herself to high school from her father's place in another town. Once armed with a plan, her moves became swift. Rest assured, they were not sudden in her mind.

One of the more troubling aspects of our story is how I was so self-absorbed that I could not see any of this coming. I knew we fought. I often knew I was wrong and always sought to apologize after the fact. I usually knew I was angry but had no idea how long my mood lasted or what I may or may not have said or done in the heat of the moment. It was just a sensation of a fog that would set in as I calmed down. In later years my daughter would tell me that she didn't want me to know the ugliness of some of what occurred, that I would wind up and nothing could calm me down.

As I worked on myself and sought help, she was away and taking a much-needed break from her family unit. Although I was doing my best to show up differently, I was her trigger, and her reaction to me was visceral. The more I leaned into her, the more she pulled back. I watched as tables turned, and I became the recipient of *her* pent-up emotions. At first, I took it personally until I realized that I was reaping what I had sown. She was mirroring my own actions back to me. I had unwittingly taught her this method of communication, and as she found peace away from me, her resolution to take a different path and heal herself took hold.

She had given many early years of unconditional support and love to me. She now needed to turn that inward and focus on herself. After years of walking on eggshells, avoiding my calls, and arm's-length interactions, she made a formal break with me and called me to let me know. Remarkably, on that call, I *still* didn't realize it was the last time I would hear her voice for a very long time. It was then that I forged ahead again, back into therapy, and began a journey of self-discovery to understand my part in this situation. I wanted to learn to not only accept what she had chosen, but also to align with her and love her unconditionally. I needed to understand how I could behave in such a mean-spirited way to someone I loved the most in the world.

It doesn't take living in a literal war zone to create lasting, negative impact or trauma in children's lives. The things around us can trigger or exacerbate the traits we inherit. We may inadvertently create generational trauma by passing down emotional and mental and/or physical trauma, including self-destructive or co-dependent tendencies, especially if we measure ourselves against skewed yardsticks. My mission is to create awareness that seemingly "normal" children may struggle with trauma and undiagnosed mental illness spurred on by their environment, and it can be catastrophic.

Family is a beautiful thing when it's healthy, but when the dynamic is toxic, the expectation for children to maintain devout loyalty to the unit at any cost can cause lasting detrimental effects, sometimes leading children to experience loneliness, despair, hopelessness, rage, or total disconnect. Without a proper outlet or understanding, kids can turn on *themselves* and form self-loathing tendencies that follow them into their adult lives and impact everything around them.

I want to speak to the generation raised by "The Greatest Generation"— *my* generation. I loved my parents dearly, to a fault, but sometimes they weren't so great. Unintentionally, they may have conveyed unhealthy thought patterns because it was all they knew. These messages became the barometers by which I measured my own self-development, worth, beliefs, and choices.

Mental health is a current hot topic—it is on the world's mind as we face suicide rates and diagnoses of depression, anxiety, and mood disorders rising at unprecedented levels. If underlying trauma manifests alongside other issues and diseases, it can create a circular, top-down treatment of symptoms rather than addressing the root cause from the inside out, as was my case. People can lose years of their lives by being misdiagnosed, mistreated, and misunderstood. From my vantage point, as someone who is more than halfway through this life, I can confidently say the faces of trauma, depression, and anxiety often go unrecognized, even though there are treatments and knowledge available today that were hushed or buried in ignorance years ago. On what basis do I substantiate this claim? I am the proof, along with thousands of others like me who push on every day, trying to solve for the equation that equals inner-peace. We ARE the proof.

Someone with suppressed trauma and mental illness will often wear a "mask"—a carefully crafted public "face" attempting to remain connected and accepted, but this mask can be suffocating and oppressive. It represents pushing through the shame and lack of acknowledgment, fear of judgment, loathing of self, and feelings of accompanying guilt and unworthiness. Is it any wonder why so many people struggle to manifest a fulfilling, satisfying life? *The inner conflict will never allow it.* Worst of all, such unresolved turmoil can contribute to the crumbling of relationships and lives.

It may not have been my fault, but it WAS my responsibility to fix it.

I didn't fix it. I neither recognized the need to fix anything, nor did I have the tools to do so. Instead, I created almost identical circumstances. Sadly, this is not an uncommon phenomenon. Freud referred to it as "repetition compulsion," a neurotic defense mechanism used as an attempt to rewrite history. It's deep, but in a nutshell, the child tries to no avail to please an emotionally unstable or unavailable parent, believing the situation is their own fault. Since the issue lies within the parent and *not* the child, there can be no resolution. Now an adult, this person has an unhealthy pattern of behavior running unconsciously in their mind, with their "inner-child" still seeking to fill the void. Symbolic stand-ins for the parent can be lovers, spouses, even children. In this way, the patterns can repeat and behaviors can be passed down. A childhood environment filled with chaos, instability, and traumatic experiences left me full of suppressed rage and feeling inadequate to make and trust my own decisions as an adult. By the time I figured my shit out, it was far too late to put the shattered pieces of my life back together, or undo the damage done in the lives of my children. In the spirit of recognizing patterns of behavior and early warning signs, I unpack my life's details in the following chapters. I make no excuses for myself now, but I had plenty then.

Many of my friends and their parents believe cutting off family to be the most egregious act they can imagine. They believe it is self-serving behavior. Are today's young adults more selfish? Compared to the blind allegiance my generation had toward our parents despite toxic home environments, it may seem that they are. I believe, because our kids have learned how to protect themselves and break the chain of intergenerational trauma, they will improve their own health and their relationships for generations of people to come.

How? By creating healthy environments for themselves, they will make it possible to produce a consistent pattern of happy, well-adjusted children. Several young women I spoke with chose not to have kids out of fear of passing down traits or genes that could perpetuate mental illness or generational trauma. That's not selfish. That's selfless.

I hate that my own role in this dramatic shift has left me on the outside of my daughter's life. I have struggled to reconcile myself to her choices, and have felt like it would kill me most days, but I finally understand it. These young women and men, including my own daughter, took drastic measures to protect themselves and those yet to come by breaking the cycle the only way they knew how. They don't wish to "punish" their parents; they simply want to heal themselves and protect anyone else they bring into their adult lives.

They share a common belief that this shit ends with them.

If you are a young adult reading this, and your parent or parents exhibited emotional instability, I am profoundly sorry. I can't bear to see it now that I am aware of the implications such an experience has on a young life. If I could reach through this page and hold you for a moment, I would. I would tell you that you didn't deserve it, it shouldn't have occurred. I would tell you that you are worthy of having a happy, whole life. I would encourage you to seek therapy, practice compassion, and work on self-love. I would say to you, with your face held gently in my hands, "You matter. On behalf of every parent who let you down, you deserved better."

If you are a parent and know the isolating sting of regret from emotionally wounding your child or children, perhaps even driving them to estrangement, I would hold you, too. Not because what you did was acceptable, because we both know it wasn't. I would do so because likely inside of you is your wounded inner-child, a child who desperately needed guidance, love, foundation, acceptance, or treatment of another kind and didn't get it. But you know what? You can figure this out now.

Even if you realize we are all victims of victims, how does one move for-
ward from the inner torment of knowing they hurt the ones they loved
most at the same time they were hurting themselves?

Think about a drunk driver who hits another car, causing harm or killing
the person in the other vehicle. Of course, the offender deserves punishment
for driving while intoxicated. The intoxicated driver didn't intentionally
set out to harm anyone (they were intoxicated), yet they are indisputably
responsible for the damage they caused. Additionally, they must live with
the outcome of their choice for the rest of their lives. While it's tempting to
think they deserve to rot in jail and think about their actions, I invite you to
consider that we all wound people, sometimes killing their spirits. We may
not be vehicular felons, but the power of the unbridled tongue, suppressed
rage, fear, anxiety, depression, and instability can all cause unintentional
harm. Living with the unforeseen consequences of our actions is often the
stiffest penalty we can pay. Learning to understand why we or someone
else may have acted in a certain way, the cycle of abuse, and the antidote of
forgiveness can help us to lessen the pain and move forward, inch by inch.

You can be on either side of the coin or on both sides of it, as the now-adult
child victimized by parents, and/or as a parent who finally recognizes they
wounded their child and does not understand why it occurred. Some parents
fail to realize just how screwed up some of their messaging and behavior
is. It's a crapshoot, and we must find a way for more positive outcomes to
prevail. Many adult children don't understand that their parents were also
victims themselves.

Even if they do understand the idea of generational trauma, the price
these children paid sometimes leads them to make extreme choices to find
healing and form some semblance of a happy life, often cutting themselves

off from their family of origin. When that happens—and it seems to be happening more frequently—we now see a fragmented population and two generations clashing with no soft skills to understand each other. In the wake of our heightened awareness of this phenomenon, the younger generation may be perceived as over-correcting, and the older generation may become stuck reliving the consequences of their misguided actions. This leaves little room for *either* generation to adequately heal even though the physical separation is in place.

After over a year of no contact with my daughter, and strained relationships with others resulting from another bout of depression and anxiety spurred by the estrangement, I knew it was time to take a deep dive into examining the patterns of my past, work on forgiving myself, and set about healing my heart by helping others who are in a similar situation. I share some of what worked for me in this book.

My daughter could have placated me with an arm's-length relationship and occasional niceties. I assure you that if she had not cut me off entirely, I wouldn't have been sufficiently motivated to dig deeper, to try to gain insight into what happened to me, to her, and to the countless others who grapple with this taboo subject.

It's the world's worst breakup.

CHAPTER 2

Purpose In The Pain

During the initial phase of no contact from my daughter, there were days I felt I had survived the worst of it, and nights I would lie in bed, sleepless, crying, praying, and begging not to have to face another day. It's hard to feel like you're living your best life when you lose a child to an intentionally severed relationship. I wanted relief from the non-stop distressed thoughts in my head.

One time, during a Zoom call with a specialist who dealt with childhood trauma and PTSD, I cried through an entire box of tissues while my nose bled profusely for thirty minutes, as she watched, horrified. As the blood ran unchecked down my face, she asked me three times if I should see a doctor. I replied that the nosebleeds happened frequently, and I just didn't care enough about myself to call anyone.

Was I suicidal? The answer is both yes and no. Yes, to the degree that if God came down and said it was time for me to go, I would have lunged at the chance. There were times that I fantasized about saving someone's life at the expense of my own so that I could end things in a dignified, respectful way. *There, I've said it.* And no, in that I know suicide doesn't stop the pain—it merely passes it on. I have passed on enough pain to the people I love to last three lifetimes. I refuse to pass on any more. No one we love should ever wonder if they could have intervened or helped. That belief has kept me grounded and swinging my legs out of bed every day.

As I vacillated between the varying emotions after my daughter disengaged, I learned to accept each shift for what it was—*impermanent.* The very nature of the ups and downs of healing should continually give us comfort, knowing that every new day brings with it the chance of a different scenario from the day before. My goal was to develop the habit of focusing on the good experiences that occur daily, so the painful things didn't overwhelm me. Putting a process and framework in place to override my emotions and feelings helped. It may sound mechanical, but nothing else was moving the needle, and my life was spinning out of control. I tried medication, countless self-help books, psychologists, coaches, training programs, and hypnosis. While all were helpful to a point, it wasn't until I learned to detach from the outcome I wanted that I began to experience some relief. I accepted my situation and eased into my commitment to self-love and forgiveness. Learning to let go of the need to control life, rather than fight for control over it, was the ultimate lesson.

It's not easy to always be positive, especially if you deal with something as difficult as estrangement, but neutral is attainable, so I learned to embrace it.

When we experience long stretches of sadness, feeling overwhelmed, or depressed states, it's easy to forget what being happy feels like. When you don't remember it, you can't embody it. It's like drawing a bow back hard and strong, only to find no target. How can you possibly release the arrow and attempt to hit a bullseye with nothing to aim for? Since depressive episodes can be triggered by circumstances *or* be the result of a chemical imbalance, evaluation by a trained professional and/or medication and therapy may be in order to achieve meaningful results. In my case, for example, I found that I could become habituated to situational sadness and the more I marinated in it, the more I sought validation to feel it. I had to learn to recognize when this was happening, allow myself to accept the sadness for a brief period, and then take action to break the behavior pattern before it became ingrained. It required determined and intentional work, but I learned that I truly had the ability to make such changes once I was ready.

It's still a battle some days, as I see constant reminders of my life's deficits directly related to my actions. The situations sometimes seem too insurmountable to unwind. Decades of holding worry, insomnia, grief, and inner-turmoil started taking a toll on my physical body. I needed to learn the importance of self-care, the value of small habits, better boundaries, and creating a neutral space inside myself. Now I move forward, knowing the lessons are invaluable to me, and—hopefully—to others. I've pledged to give a voice to those who are hurting and to find a purpose in the pain. If I can do that, if my story finds others like me so they will know they aren't alone, I will have accomplished something of value.

My public persona always hid the mess inside. Despite outward appearances, I went through life often feeling isolated and in deep pain. I had respectable jobs, dressed and acted professionally, and appeared gregarious and happy. Considered generally warm and kind by my peers, I'd encourage mostly everyone around me, except myself. Even though I was able to function "normally" at work, no matter how hard I tried, I couldn't stop over-complicating my life and lashing out at home with my family. The self-imposed stress often led me to make irrational or impulsive decisions that I would later regret, resulting in still more sadness and anger. The details changed, but the patterns of behavior remained the same. I was aware of the trauma, but there had to be more to it. Otherwise, it seemed as though I was simply a mean-spirited bitch who didn't care, and I knew that wasn't me—at least I didn't want that to be me.

I realized that in addition to self-loathing and guilt, which could *only* co-create undesirable circumstances in my life, my wiring was off. I believe had I received competent professional help when I was young, I may have been able to learn how to address my trauma and emotional issues, and developed coping skills from an earlier age so perhaps I would not have become so angry with myself. This realization cracked the door just enough for self-compassion to seep in, which was a game-changer.

Layering trauma atop any other undiagnosed mental or emotional illness is like mixing kindling with kerosene, at least in my case. A trigger becomes a match, and once struck, entire lives can go up in flames if not properly managed. Armed with my newfound understanding about self-compassion, I found productive ways to counteract the recriminating labels for things I had struggled with from early childhood. I learned to assess whether I was born with a tendency to lash out, develop depression, anxiety, and rumination, and to understand that everything was enhanced by childhood trauma.

For me, it's less important to understand why, and more impactful to be able to give myself a break. I dealt with issues that exacerbated the anger and depression I faced as a young adult. I demonized myself for alienating people, talking too much, constant worrying, and not regulating my emotions after my mother's death. Well-meaning and not so well-meaning people would offer advice about all sorts of things they knew little about, and I spent over twenty years thinking I was crazy, someone to be ashamed of, not worthy, and broken beyond repair. This mindset made me ripe for poor partners—the low-hanging fruit of life—and perpetuated my belief that I didn't deserve anything good. When good things occasionally found me, they were unfamiliar; I had no idea how to deal with them, so, I would self-destruct.

I still experience frustration when I think about the years spent trying to fix things with incorrect tools. When one is building a wooden box, for example, a hammer, nails, saw, and possibly some glue are generally required; but a screwdriver or wrench will not accomplish the task.

We must do the inner-work, but we need the correct tools in our tool kit to do it properly.

Sustained stress is rising in homes that look good on the outside. The glamorization of multi-tasking and over-scheduling, the often-lacking support in single-parent families, poor or infrequent stress-release, and lack of coping skills create a slippery slope. Add on the possibility of depression, anxiety, or other overlooked disorders, and home may not be where the heart is, but where the tension is. Young children exposed to such environments can experience potential structural changes within their brains. Their parents, many of whom survived trauma or are coping with mental illness themselves, may lack the self-regulation needed to calm, soothe, and meet their kids' needs.

When parents remain unable to regulate their own emotional state, the child picks up on it, and the two begin a destructive dance, bouncing off each other's negative energy, expectations, and emotions. Children do their best to adapt to their parents' behavior, but when it isn't healthy, consistent, or perceived by the child as safe, dysregulation—difficulty managing emotional responses—can occur. Instead, responses can become exaggerated, often falling outside acceptable norms. Ineffective attachment patterns can form and follow these kids into adulthood, potentially mirroring the parent's destructive behaviors and perpetuating the unhealthy cycle for yet another generation.

In his book, *The Body Keeps the Score: Brain, Mind, and Body in the Healing of Trauma*, psychiatrist, author, and educator Dr. Bessel Van Der Kolk, M.D. writes in detail about the varying degrees of dysregulation and attachment issues many children develop within homes where sustained domestic or emotional abuse, disengagement, anxiety, or overwhelm is present with the primary caregiver. When children don't feel safe, they have trouble regulating their moods and responses, and psychological issues can develop over time.

Dr. Van Der Kolk writes, "Parents who are preoccupied with their own trauma, such as domestic abuse, or rape, or the recent death of a parent or sibling, may also be too emotionally unstable and inconsistent to offer much comfort and protection (to the child). While all parents need all the help they can get to raise secure children, traumatized parents, in particular, need help to learn how to become attuned and responsive to their children's needs." Sometimes, the parent-child roles become reversed, with the parent leaning heavily on the child for emotional stability, as was often the case in my dynamic with my daughter. Children subjected to parents who display moodiness or extreme personalities may tell themselves it isn't *that* bad. Looking back, I didn't recognize my daughter's reclusive and challenging behaviors as warning signs that something was wrong with *me*. Often self-absorbed, I was impossible to approach, with low self-esteem and an inability to take any criticism, constructive or otherwise. It was a no-win situation for my daughter and me.

Children believe in us and the stories we live out. Typically compassionate by nature, they try to help, fix, and take on our emotions, pain, and anxiety. They only want to please us. This lasts for a while until they are older and have a wider basis for comparing what other healthy homes look like, what teachers say at school, and what their friends experience. They may have a "WTF?" moment when they realize they are getting shortchanged. They often find "replacement parents," other adults who can provide a nurturing, loving environment, advice, and normalcy.

Amazingly, trauma can be caused by a one-time event, often leading adults to minimize its impact on the child, leaving it undiagnosed.

My mother's attempted suicide and my father's sudden death spurred worry, guilt, anxiety, depression, and lasting trauma before I was ten years old. I forged a strong but unhealthy bond with my mom. She loved me but infiltrated my thoughts, demeanor, and expectations with her versions of the truth, which were often skewed. Even as an older adult when I should have known better, I still had a strong urge to please and fix her. Beyond loving her, I *idolized* her. She was my primary source of affection, yet she simultaneously ruled in a dominant, harsh, and ignorant way, which was all she knew to do. I grew up thinking people could scream, yell, hit, be depressed, throw tantrums, hold grudges, say hurtful things, fight unfairly, and everyone around them would deal with *and* get over it. In those days, we didn't acknowledge or treat emotional issues. Strep throat or swimmer's ear might merit a doctor's visit, but aside from that, it was "Quit whining," "Toughen up," or "Keep your mouth shut and be thankful." In my childhood home, we got beatings "if needed," and then we just got on with our shit.

I lacked awareness of how screwed up this kind of environment was and never developed the courage to do what my daughter eventually did, disconnect and break the cycle.

Instead, triggered by my mother's death, I became angry, short-tempered, hostile, disconnected, and depressed. The more the long-suppressed negative emotions emerged, the more people in my life pulled away. I was 28, and my daughter was two, and neither one of us had any idea what was about to transpire. It was easier to blame others than to take a close look at was festering inside me.

I had stuffed my mixed emotions down for decades and I had no idea what to do with them once they surfaced. They erupted, cascading around me. Like violent storms, there was no predicting when one would come, how long it would linger, or when it would blow over. All anyone—usually my kids—could do was hunker down and hope for the swift passing.

What profound damage those unreconciled parts of me did to my life. I manifested the worst of me right when I needed to be at my best, leaving "life-shrapnel" all around me.

Don't assume there is only one person inside you. We are *all* comprised of parts—light and dark, substance, and shadow. When the pieces inside us don't reconcile well, the whole of who we are suffers, keeping the best version of ourselves from the world. When integrated and proactively treated, though, our facets can shine like diamonds. Most people do eventually find ways of incorporating themselves as they gain experience and wisdom, but *some don't*. Without proper treatment and counseling, suffering becomes silent inner torment. Worse, when combined with poor "emotional hygiene," it can cause significant collateral damage.

I continued to live my life as a victim well into adulthood. I remained in a perpetual state of "woe is me," waiting for other people to rescue or fix me, while I projected my inner-wounds onto the world like an endless filmstrip. It took many years of my life to understand that we shut out seeing things through others' eyes when we always see ourselves as the victim. As a victim, we may see people as not engaging, not supportive, difficult or being disrespectful. The reality may be that we emit negative energy, seeking guidance more than we should. A lack of confidence in our decision making or personal authority may leave constant drama swirling around us. We may take on other traits as we spin the story of disconnect in our heads, leading to a vicious, self-fulfilling cycle.

A victim always blames external circumstances for internal conflict.

Eventually and thankfully, I sought treatment, first symptomatically, and then—later—for help in identifying the root cause of my symptoms: trauma. The diagnosis of PTSD was the starting point of healing and accountability for following a poorly designed blueprint which dictated my choices and subsequent outcomes, and negatively impacted my children. But my ego, ignorance, and the limiting belief that seeking treatment was for weak people kept me from getting the help I needed until I was in my forties.

When I asked one of my brothers for details that I couldn't recall for this book, his immediate reaction was one of disdain. "Why are you so bent on living in the past?" He wanted to know if I sought my daughter's sympathy and reminded me that people with situations far worse than mine made great things out of their lives. Stunned, I replied the last thing I was looking for was sympathy. He told me that he believed I could have made better choices as an adult, mainly related to behaving like our mother. While I agreed with his premise, I tried to explain that I had felt utterly incapable at the time. He challenged me, stating that he and our other brother managed to do so, implying that I should have been able to as well. I replied that our deceased brother, who struggled with a lifetime of anger and alcohol abuse, clearly did not. It was a frustrating and futile conversation.

This kind of judgment motivated me to write and share my story. Not everyone can make the right choices, even though they may have had the opportunity. Most people generally make the best choices they are able to make given their unique circumstances in that moment. As we learn more (sometimes from the fallout of our choices), we gradually get better at making decisions. Also, we don't know how any particular child will respond after facing traumatic childhood experiences or undiagnosed disorders. This isn't an excuse; it's a fact. Once armed with knowledge and a way to move forward, the choice to *remain* a victim or an asshole becomes an excuse. We need to shine the light on and heal the pain while simultaneously learning to reframe our stories.

When we stop identifying with our inner victim, we are at liberty to become the hero we seek.

In finance, some experts rely on information referred to as leading or lagging indicators. It's data that will either forecast changes to come or display patterns and trends of what is, after the fact. Our lives are a lagging indicator, an accumulation of the small choices and decisions we have made along the way. My mother said, "Wherever you are at age fifty is where you will stay"—somber words to swallow. I believe she was trying to convey that fifty years of habits, behaviors, and decision-making processes are hard to change. I have learned that it's not, however, impossible. She was wrong, even though she was trying to teach me an important point. There are treatments, resources, and brain-hacks available today that we knew nothing about years ago. In addition to the promising research we see in neuroscience, studies also show the importance of our energetic vibration and mindset, which can hasten our physical and emotional healing. This is why it's uncharitable, and potentially very harmful, to pass judgment on the choices people make early in their lives when their options for choosing differently were likely much more restricted.

CHAPTER 3

Bad Blueprints

Once I became a parent, instead of remembering how I felt being treated harshly as a kid, all that remained was the blueprint of doing the same. This is the essence of how behaviors can be passed down. Without tapping into my feelings from childhood, I lacked the understanding of how *my* child felt as I dictated what I wanted. It was a total lack of empathy, reprehensible behavior on my part, and it was modeled from the most formative years of my life onward.

Like so many families, my family was disjointed at best and often plagued with hostility and anger. My siblings and I would joke as adults about our mother's "fits" or outrageous antics, like when she burned all the boys' stuffed animals and toys in a fire. But the stories lost their humor as I saw the emergence of my own toxic personality. My nature was practically identical—erratic, reactive, impulsive, and unnecessarily harsh.

I was seven years younger than my youngest brother and we had two older brothers as well. My parents never seemed happy, and the madness that occurred on an almost daily basis would sound like fiction if I got into the detail of it all. We all lived amid an undercurrent of tension, usually mounting into some type of explosion between my mother, father, and brothers. My mom was prone to fits of rage and dissatisfaction, and she had an overly critical view of others.

Dad blended quietly into the background, keeping the peace, which only seemed to enrage my mother more. The boys would often get into massive fights with my parents and each other, and it was not unusual for neighbors to call the police—the fights were that bad. It made me nervous, edgy, uptight, and frequently sad. It was so intense at times that my middle brother or his girlfriend would whisk me out of the house and take me someplace, anyplace else. I was always thankful for the rescue, and when we returned home, mom would act as if nothing had even happened. It was bizarre to me.

My mother would often overreact with me, even when I was very young. One grade-school night I asked to stay up late to watch a *Peanuts* special on TV. One of my brothers quickly reminded her about something I'd done earlier, which pissed her off, so I snapped at him, "Just leave me alone, dammit!" I didn't even know what I was saying because I heard it all the time. She was furious because we had family in the kitchen, and I had used a curse word.

Someone made comments about my mouth, fueling her anger. She went to smack me, and instinctively I put my hands up by my face. Screaming that I raised my hands to her, she slapped me anyway and sent me to my room for the night. Sobbing uncontrollably, I went back downstairs to explain that I didn't want my face to get hit since I had school pictures the next day. I begged for another chance to watch the show, but she stood, unrelenting, while my grandparents, aunts, and uncles sat at the table, smoking and talking as if nothing odd was happening. My brother just laughed at me.

It was a "children should be seen and not heard" mentality, and she was trying to do the right thing by keeping me in line. But instead, her behavior increased the hostility between my brother and me, and reinforced the notion that parents were supposed to dominate their children. I went off to bed, missing "The Great Pumpkin" and hardly sleeping a wink. My photo from that school year captured so much sadness in my eyes that I later tore it up because it hurt to look at it.

Much to my mother's chagrin, I was also a tomboy, and girly things didn't interest me. My long golden mane was often the only way to distinguish my gender amid my rough-and-tumble traits. I loved to climb trees, catch frogs, get dirty, and often neglected my hair, leaving it tangled and unkempt. Over and over, she would tell me to brush it or cut it off, and because I was a kid, I rarely listened. I didn't brush my teeth regularly back then, either. What was she going to do, pull them out of my mouth?

Mom got her tresses washed and set weekly, and I usually tagged along. Her hair was of such importance that she would often sleep with toilet paper wrapped around it at night or use a satin pillowcase to ensure it stayed perfect. The salon was adjacent to a bowling alley where I would kill time playing video games or putting balls back on the big, round racks. Sometimes the lady behind the snack bar would give me a soda or a cookie, and I always looked forward to my visits.

One Saturday, we arrived at the salon for mom's standing appointment, and I was scheduled for my hair to be washed and "trimmed" for my Holy Communion the next day. I happily obliged, hopping onto the bolstered chair, chatting away in oblivion. Suddenly, I felt the cold metal scissors close to my ear, and before I could question it, I heard a snip. I watched a huge chunk of my waist-length hair fall to the floor and screamed in horror, "STOP! That's my hair!" It was too late.

Mom stood by while the woman cooed how pretty I would look and how much easier it would be to take care of. I sobbed the entire time, fidgeting in my chair that no longer faced the mirror. When it was done, I had shorter hair than either of my three brothers. I was speechless. We ran an errand before going home, and the salesman referred to me as her son. The next day, I stood amid all the little girls with swept-up hair and fancy curls flowing from beneath their communion veils, wishing I would disappear. I shredded those photos when I was an adult.

I became used to my mother's harsh and erratic actions, anticipating them and often believing I brought them on. She never wanted to hurt her hand while hitting me, grabbing *anything* within reach—a shoe, vacuum cleaner pole, bread knife, belt, guitar strap—chasing me as I ran. If I tried to hold her back, it would fuel the fire. I would never dare touch her and assumed it was normal in hot-headed Italian families like mine. Yet, this same woman would gently stroke my hair while I sat with my head on her lap, kiss and hug me, and I never once doubted her love.

While these incidents are mild compared to children who suffer from sexual and physical abuse, that is the very point. I talk about "covert" behaviors that impact many children and remain unaddressed in a future chapter, "Sneaky Truths." Unfortunately, these conflicting and confusing messages can be destructive and were the foundation on which my inner structure was built.

I mean no disrespect to anyone, but it's precisely why stories like this don't get told. Part of me feels guilty writing about this because, at the same time, my mother was a caring, *wonderful* woman who deeply loved her kids and family. The juxtaposition of the two sets of feelings I had toward her often made me feel confused. On the one hand, I was overwhelmed and upset, and on the other, I felt so loved and special.

I learned to equate love with volatility, and as all little children do, absorbed the patterns of behavior I observed every day.

I spent hours alone in my room each day to escape, read, write, play with dolls, and interview each one. I'd ask my "friends" how they felt about being in my house and assure them they would always be safe. We would "talk" about what made them feel scared or happy, and if they believed in God, or what they wanted to do when they grew up. In character, I would always answer on their behalf. With its pink walls and red wool carpet, my little haven became my hiding place and safe space.

My favorite "friend" was a hand-sewn frog stuffed with beans that a kind neighbor made for me. They were from the South, polite, and soft-spoken. I would wander over to their house just about any time I could to soak up its normalcy. When I was around seven, they moved away, but they made Kermit for me before leaving, and I adored him. I didn't realize I was associating him with them. I don't recall what became of him or any of my doll friends from back then. I just know that each represented the people in my life, and in my room, I made things happen as I wanted because it was *my* stage.

Unfortunately, the stages we share with others in real life have a way of defining our roles.

Often our lives are scripted out, and characters cast without our willing participation. We don't know any better as we grow into adulthood, so we go along for the ride unless we figure out how to make better choices and changes. To adapt, I pushed through many challenging circumstances on the way to adulthood, but I wasn't prepared for any of them. I never knew how to regulate my state or understand what my triggers were as I faced them. I propelled myself into responsibilities I was ill-equipped to handle, like marriage and family, because I believed that was what I was supposed to do with my life. It was all that was ever discussed and encouraged as my path forward. It was as if one half of my brain knew what to do, and the other half was underdeveloped in the appropriate expression of feelings and expectations. I could successfully mirror others in earlier years, but when faced with the typical family challenges and poor spousal communication, my responses were exaggerated.

Now, rather than continue to probe for answers, I strive for acceptance of my situation without the need to control it. The monster within, while still egregiously wrong, may not have had as much control over itself as I once thought. I hope someday that I can say I forgive myself *entirely* as, without that forgiveness, my life cannot unfold in the best way possible.

CHAPTER 4

One Tough Mother

Environment plays a role in what we absorb at young ages and how we perceive the world. When we lack certainty or emotional support as children, those emotions lie dormant inside of us. We may unwittingly form behavior patterns that can run the gamut from mildly to excessively abusive. I won't say that my mother intended to hurt anyone because I don't believe she did. If I could time-travel back to *her* mother's life growing up, I bet I'd see patterns of emotional wounds that played a role in her responses to her children. This lets my grandmother off the hook, too, as she also did the best she could with what she knew.

So, was my mother a perpetrator or a victim? She was both, like me.

As I write *my* version of this story, I love my mother deeply, even after years of feeling what I thought was hatred after she died. Like me, she was unable to control *her* beast within once it was triggered. Was it from menopause, mental illness, trauma, narcissistic traits, compulsivity, low self-esteem, people-pleasing, a need to be heard, or just ego? I will never know which combination impacted her. As such, I am giving her Grace. That's my choice. I will defend her from the judgment so quickly delivered and understand that she had no coping tools and only her own faulty blueprint to follow.

It doesn't make my childhood experience okay, but holding anger or resentment toward her will *never* serve me. At the end of the day, on her death bed, she died knowing she loved her kids very much and screwed it up terribly. I sometimes wonder if I won't endure a similar fate. That is enough retribution for any soul to experience, and I pray she is at peace now, knowing she was indeed loved.

Growing up, we always had a nice home, nice cars, and my parents apparently maintained a lifestyle beyond their means. I was too young to understand or notice. At one point, they turned two of the upstairs bedrooms into a makeshift apartment, complete with a kitchenette. Mom's intrusive nature quickly brought the rental arrangement to an end, along with the extra household income. The space stayed vacant for a while, and eventually, it was turned back into bedrooms, but the appliances remained.

One morning I heard mom yelling about something before I left for school, so I snuck out the side door to avoid getting caught in the middle and missing my bus. I knew she would be pissed, but it was the lesser of two evils.

When I came home, she wasn't in the kitchen like she usually was, so I went upstairs to look for her. As I reached the top of the steps, I was hit with a terrible odor. She was in the spare room, passed out on the bed with the oven door open, billowing gas. My heart pounded as I shook her, yelling for her to wake up. She was groggy, but alive. I slammed the oven door, turned off the gas, and called for my brother. Eventually, she came around. Later that night, her older sister comforted her by saying menopause was the culprit. No one suggested she seek professional help, nor did we discuss what occurred.

The next day, she kept me home from school, and I sat with my head on her lap as she lovingly stroked my hair. She and my uncle told me Mom wasn't feeling well, and it was none of anyone's business at school. This taught me that acknowledging and dealing with depression, fear, or anger was not what tough people did. They just pushed it down, moved on, and never spoke about it again. Decades later, when I asked my brother about it, he said she did it as a ruse, to get attention, and was never in any real danger. But, at that time, I was scared to death, and I don't think anyone around me realized what an experience like that does to a child.

I became even more nervous and anxious, lost sleep, exhibited hyperactive and defiant behavior, hid boxes of Twinkies underneath my bed, and ate them to calm myself down. Whenever I would have a meltdown, she would scold me and say, "Big girls don't cry, and we can never use a crutch in life." I believed her. Amid the constant chaos, she'd somehow comfort me, and oddly enough, I grew up feeling very loved by her. Criticized, scared, and never good enough, but loved.

She always looked like she had it all together, turned heads, and commanded attention when she entered a room. Always polished, with a polarizing personality, people either loved or hated her. Fierce, beautiful, loving, and smart, she was beloved by my friends, extended family, her employees, and grandchildren. She also had an incredibly generous spirit. Self-described as too skinny and gawky in school, she exhibited extreme vanity, she puffed herself up with her persona, outwardly appearing bold and confident. As I look back, though, I believe she struggled inside. Her self-esteem was not what I thought.

Her life was punctuated by her strict, authoritarian style that always demanded more, and she could unleash the fury of a hurricane when upset. Volatile and unpredictable, she once tossed our Thanksgiving Day turkey into the garbage after an argument with my dad. She stormed out, taking me with her; we went to see 101 Dalmatians in the movie theater. I was just a little kid and didn't understand what was happening. I was sad about the fight but happy about the film. When we returned, Dad had cleaned up the entire table, and we all acted as if nothing had happened. She would often do things like that, and although she may have felt regret, I don't think I ever heard an apology come from her lips.

Driven and never satisfied, she pushed herself and everyone around her with her perfectionist tendencies. I once woke at 2:00 a.m. to see the red embers of a cigarette in the corner of the pitch-black living room. "Mom, is that you?" I asked. Sitting in a chair, she let out a heavy sigh and told me to go back to bed. She had purchased new drapes made of heavy fabric and had just finished ironing and putting the last one up. She would never stop a project until it was finished, no matter how exhausting or unnecessary it seemed to anyone else. Her list of things to accomplish seemed endless, and—I believe—contributed to her inner burn-out. She kept herself in a constant state of motion, likely running from her own demons, which is the ultimate distraction from oneself. I would learn this truth the hard way as an adult.

Early in life, I was her toy and joy, the only girl amid four men who drove her crazy, but eventually, the years of strife and tension started to show in my demeanor, too. I was often at odds with the youngest of my brothers, and our fights became more regular as my actions became more hostile toward him.

I also had little use for my eldest brother, who was always doing frightening things, like when he threw a picnic table bench at the kitchen window at my mother and me. I stood there staring blankly, in a state of disbelief. Once, he even held a gun (we found out later it wasn't loaded) to my other brother's head in a fit of rage, threatening to make his wife a widow. There were issues, but we just let it roll.

Looking back at the relationships within my mother's family, the same tox-icity that infected our household was commonplace. Her mother was the matriarch, and pleasing her was always top of mind at any cost. Planning my wedding, I had my heart set on a blush-pink dress. My mother barked, "Your grandmother will think you are pregnant!" despite my 22-inch waist, and forbade me to purchase it. It caused such a fight that I succumbed, ordering a bright, white dress. Mom had chosen a stunning black dress for herself, but when my grandmother quipped that it seemingly mourned my impending marriage, she quickly exchanged it for cream, despite my pro-tests and her disappointment. She and her mother had the same dynamic I had with her: the co-dependent child trying to please a parent who could never be satisfied.

My grandmother's harsh, critical behaviors frustrated my mom, yet she con-tinued to engage, seeking out the validation she craved and never received. She and her twin sister were often at odds over their mother and would go long periods without speaking. It was as if all her siblings were pitted against each other through the years, with little care taken for long-term repercussions. The family spent time together, yet it seemed more out of habit than anything, especially in later years. Lashing out in anger was an unintentional communication style, and not something viewed as prob-lematic or worth trying to change.

My mother mellowed considerably with age and was eventually diagnosed with lung cancer, a slow-growing mass she ignored, hiding the constant coughing. It wasn't until I noticed several empty bottles of cough syrup in the trash, full ones in her cabinet, and her reluctance to walk short dis-tances or climb steps that I badgered her to go to the doctor, but by then it was far too late.

I spent the last two weeks of her life sitting by her hospital bed in a plastic chair, thinking about why she had refused to address it. We talked about life, and she told me not to wait until I was sixty years old to calm down. I believe part of her was ready to leave the messy life she had created. I would be lying if I said that I haven't sometimes felt that way myself. I was devastated when she died just months after her diagnosis.

After her death, I heard stories that made my hair stand on end about her over-disciplining my brothers when they were kids and the outrageous things she did. These revelations served to explain much of the resentment they exhibited toward her. She was physical, and often embarrassed or punished them severely for small offenses. In one memorable incident, she threw a brick at the windshield of a car that was on the driveway because my brother wouldn't clean up the area around it quickly enough. She screamed that her driveway was not an auto repair shop. It was non-stop conflict with an overreaction to *everything*.

In the absence of that historical understanding, I felt disconnected and angry toward my brothers for most of my younger years. I had defended my mother at any cost. Hearing the stories and details of her behavior felt to me like tearing off Superman's cape. When these stories about her came out after her death, I was forced to deal with a new perception of her. She was far worse with them than she ever was to me, and yet, they managed to compartmentalize it and move forward with their lives. To say this created distance between my brothers and me is an understatement. As time went on, and I manifested almost identical circumstances in my own adult life, I felt anger and resentment towards her. She wasn't alive, so I had to reconcile it all inside my mind. The more time I spent blaming her, the less time I spent looking inside myself.

Eventually, I understood she was a victim, too, and did the best she could with what she knew. It sucked, but she didn't have the skills she needed to do things better. One would think I'd have been determined to be different, but I was well into my own adulthood before I understood what had happened with my mother. Long before I reached that understanding, I embodied her and repeated the patterns and behavior that had been laid out for me. It's taken me damn near forty years to process the "whys" that occurred within my family and how intertwined our actions and reactions were.

CHAPTER 5

Daddy's Girl

In fairness, not all negative situations create self-induced limitations or manifest into behavioral issues. Many people *credit* their traumatic or painful past for shaping their resilient nature and enabling them to flourish. However, no two people are the same relative to inherited traits or negative experiences. Some make the best of the worst situations, while others make the worst of the best conditions. Most people fall somewhere between those two extremes. If you think I'm promoting excuses, please let me be clear. There are NONE. However, developmental or cognitive issues and atypical neurological wiring occurs with predictable frequency. When left undiagnosed and untended, these conditions can lead to messed up adults who then go on to mess up their own lives and the lives of others around them. Combined with other negative behaviors, it can set a person's life on fire, and not in a good way.

Too often, images, memories, thought patterns, beliefs, and fears are transmitted into children's young minds, with caregivers oblivious to the emotional download. Being aware of impactful , traumatic events from our past is key to unlocking the limitations we may face in our present-day lives. I had already absorbed the family chaos and my mother's glossed-over attempted suicide, but little did I know the worst was yet to come.

My calm within the storm, and favorite of all, was my father. He was a quiet, understated man, and I'd do anything to be with him, including walking beside him while he cut the grass. My eyes would water from allergies, but we would spend hours talking above the mower's noisy grind, and I'd hang on his every word. In contrast to my mother, he said little, but I soaked up his calm, soothing voice when he did speak. I had scant knowledge of my father's background but knew he had been in the army and didn't grow up "in the neighborhood" like everyone else in the family. Later in life, I found out his mother was my grandfather's "second" wife. The two had an unusual relationship and I'm not sure if they ever even legally wed. That was a big deal in those days.

When my grandfather came to America, he left his "first" wife and children behind in Italy. Once in the U.S., he met my grandmother and my dad was conceived. My grandfather eventually moved his family from Italy and they lived right around the corner from my dad's childhood home. My father was, in essence, considered a "bastard" child. It was hushed, and he must have harbored so much shame that I grew up believing he was an orphan until I was an adult and found out the truth. I guess it's why my grandparents never liked him and why he idolized my mom, despite her erratic ways. Maybe all he ever wanted was to belong somewhere.

He kept late hours, and I was usually in bed by the time he got home. He'd always come to my room and tell me a bedtime story. It began the same way each night: "There once was a little girl named Bella, and she was the most beautiful little girl in the world."

Some nights I was beautiful, others smart or brave, but I was always something wonderful. He would say a few lines, and we would alternate back and forth, allowing my mind to roam, limited only by my imagination. This dialogue would continue until my eyes were so heavy with sleep that I couldn't fight it any longer.

He encouraged me to learn and challenge myself. On weekends, he would open the big red Webster's dictionary, and I would choose a random word to use in a sentence until I understood it completely. He said I needed a good vocabulary because I would be a lawyer when I grew up. I would laugh, but he assured me that I could be anything I wanted.

One night I sat up in bed, aware that several nights had gone by, and I hadn't seen him. In the morning, I asked my mother, and she said he had been working late and leaving very early, but it felt odd to me. When I went upstairs to get dressed for school, I instinctively walked into my parents' bedroom instead of mine. When I looked in the armoire where he kept his clothes, it was empty. I feverishly opened every dresser drawer, and with tears flowing down my face, I ran back downstairs into the kitchen screaming. Mom asked him to leave, and just like that, he and his things were gone.

He was living at my brother's beach house in a sleepy seashore town, and I insisted that I wanted to stay with him, crying for days until my mother allowed it. He drove up north to get me, and the entire trip back down, he tried to explain things and calm me down. The beach house had a couple of bedrooms, was situated on a lagoon, and felt peaceful and sad at the same time. We went out for dinner one chilly night, and he bought me a little white jacket from the restaurant's souvenir shop. I still have and treasure it, but feel sad when I see its tiny size.

After a few nights, I was torn, missing mom and my dogs, and became inconsolable. I had a hard time deciding where to stay. My father, sensing my overwhelm, knew I needed my routine, so he drove me back home. I don't remember how much time passed, but soon he was living with us again. I was relieved to have him there and too young to think about its permanence. I now know divine providence brought him back, and it was the last year of my life that I felt carefree.

Soon the fighting began again, and with it came the typical summer trips to the shore that mom and I would make, usually with dad staying home. Sometimes he would come down on the weekends and sometimes not, depending on the "state of their union." It was Father's Day weekend, and we were about to leave for a week-long trip without him.

I felt terrible leaving him, and something inside of me made me say, "NO!" I made such a scene on the front lawn that my mom decided to go without me since my brother was headed down the next day. But she was furious, popping the trunk of the car and grabbing my hard Samsonite suitcase. Hurling it onto the front lawn, she screamed, "I stayed home and played 'mother' on Mother's Day, so your father can play 'father' on Father's Day!" It hit the ground and broke open with such force that my clothes were strewn all about.

She took off angrily down the driveway, and I didn't know what to do other than cry. Gathering my things, I noticed one of my T-shirts snagged against the trunk of a small tree. As I reached for it, an early memory flashed in my mind as clear as day. When I was about three or four, Mom was planting the tree when I ran to her, sobbing. I had been riding my tricycle back and forth on the massive deck in the backyard when one of my brothers told me to ride down the steps. I did, dislocating my jaw so severely, it was pushed to the side of my little face. I don't recall how I got to the hospital that day, but I do remember being given a lollipop by the nurse for being such a good little girl.

How that event was available in my memory bank, triggered by my shirt on the tree, is impressive. It demonstrates the power of the brain and the stored experiences housed there. We never know when something will come up. Ironically, my jaw was the least of things that I would experience as broken, but I didn't know it yet.

CHAPTER 6

Broken Heart

My dad, worried about my mother's upset, sent my brother to the shore with her since there were no cell phones back then, nor did the house have a landline. This left just the two of us, and I couldn't have been happier. We decided to make the best of our night even though he had some chores to do. He made cut up hot dogs fried in butter so that I could eat them using chopsticks. I heard the jingle of the ice cream truck, and we sat outside in the warm summer air, eating our Creamsicles. *Orca* was on TV that night, and I pleaded to watch it. Of course, he said yes, but he needed to cut the lawn since my brother had left. He came in about halfway through mowing the backyard grass, saying he didn't feel well and needed to rest for a little while.

My movie had started, and I was huddled under my yellow crocheted blanket because the window AC unit made the room ice cold. He kissed my forehead and said I could stay up extra late if I got ready for bed. Tossing the blanket to the floor, I ran excitedly toward the stairway as he said, "I love you, Bella." I ran back to him for a hug and said, "I love you too, Daddy." Those were the last words I ever spoke to that precious man. He walked into the living room, and for a moment, I wondered why, since it had no air conditioning, but quickly dismissed it. In the time it took for me to shower, brush my teeth, and put my pajamas on, the unthinkable occurred. A blood clot had traveled to his heart, causing cardiac arrest.

As I bounced happily down the steps, I could see his reflection in the hallway mirrors. "Daddy, I'm done!" I yelled excitedly. When he didn't respond,

I assumed he was asleep. "Dad?" As I stood over him, it was clear that something was horribly wrong, even to my ten-year-old mind. His eyes were open, but they were glazed and blank, looking nowhere. I shook him, yelled, and cried, but he was unresponsive.

I knew he needed help, so I ran to the kitchen and dialed "0." I can still hear the clicking sound in my head as the rotary dial turned slowly, and the operator came on the line. I told her my name, Dad's name, our address, and that he couldn't speak or hear me. She asked me some questions and then hung up. As I ran frantically back to him, it occurred to me that I was *all alone.* Frightened, I darted back to the kitchen and dialed my aunt, who lived on the other side of town. She and my mom hadn't spoken for a while, but she was the first family member I thought to call, so I did. Dialing seven digits on a rotary phone with shaky hands felt like it took forever, but she finally answered. I explained what happened, and between her screams and tears, she said that she and my uncle were on their way.

I raced past my father again, who remained the same, then made a frantic dash out the front door screaming at the top of my lungs, hoping someone was around, but it was silent. I ran back inside and collapsed, with my head on his chest. Every so often, it would rise as if he was breathing, but the gasps for air were far apart. Unsure of what was happening, I stayed there, crying and clutching him, begging God to wake him up. Time stood still.

Unfortunately, the First Aid Squad was also on the other side of town, and by the time everyone arrived, he had gone without oxygen for too long. My brother knew CPR, but I didn't, so I couldn't help him. A man named Jay pulled me off him, and my uncle held me back as they cut his shirt open. His body jerked as the paddles hit his chest, and I kicked as hard as I could to break free because I thought they were hurting him. I watched with futile tears as they took him away on the stretcher, while I begged to go to the hospital. Instead, I was taken to my aunt's house.

I kept thinking that had I *just* behaved and gone to the shore, my brother would have been home to help him breathe. Somehow, I made it through the week but was never allowed to visit him, and I felt like my heart was ripping in half. I didn't realize he was in a coma, hooked up to life support, and my family didn't want me to see it. I don't know why they never explained it to me, even in simple terms. I might have understood, or at least felt acknowledged for the deep pain I was holding in. They were silent, and resentment, grief, guilt, and anger overwhelmed me.

One afternoon a few days later, my aunt dropped me off at my grandmother's house. I sat in the dimly lit kitchen, picking nervously at my cuticles, waiting to be picked up. The cool Formica table felt good against my face as I rested my throbbing head in silence. Eventually, my brother arrived to take me home. The car ride was oddly quiet. It occurred to me that no one had spoken much with me all day. Once home, it all became clear. Mom had decided to remove life support, and my dad passed earlier that day. I never saw him again after he was taken from the house.

Devastated to learn he was gone forever, I ran to my room and called my best friend at the time in a fit of hysteria. The youngest of my brothers heard me, took the receiver out of my hand, and placed it back onto the phone's cradle. He snapped sharply that I needed to calm down and shouldn't be carrying on to my friend the way I was. *What?* It was confusing, mean, unnecessary, and I despised him for it. I found myself wishing my brother was dead and not my father. All the other kids at school were happy because summer had officially started, but I felt numb. I don't remember much from the rest of that year except seeing my dad's coffin draped with the American flag and people milling around. I was too numb even to cry. It was like a bad dream that I couldn't wake from. No one got themselves any help, or got me any help, and I didn't know how to help myself.

I formed the belief that sharing your grief was associated with weakness, so I held it all in, as did everyone else in the house.

At barely eleven years old, I found myself tossed into full-blown puberty. Rather than the slow progression of physical changes, in a matter of a two months, my body had transformed from that of a little girl into a woman, with all the challenges associated with it. My mother took me to a doctor who said that the shock of losing my father may have spurred on such quick changes, or maybe it was just bad genetic luck. Either way, it created situations I was not prepared to deal with, as I was physically so far ahead of any of the other girls in my grade. I was gawked at for my curves and large breasts. I got my period out of the blue. I begged my mother to let me shave my legs, opting to wear long pants in the sweltering heat after hearing "No." One brother relentlessly teased me, placed my bra on the statue in the foyer, and waved a Kotex pad for all my friends to see. I felt like a freak compared to other girls and sometimes found myself in situations over my head since I looked much older. I lived with a body *far* more mature than the mind behind it.

Some of my male teachers looked at me inappropriately. An eighth-grade boy I barely knew pinned me against the wall in the stairwell, trying to shove his tongue in my mouth and grab at my breast. I jammed my knee up between his legs and ran to class, flustered and visibly shaken. I was too embarrassed to speak up, and the teacher never bothered to ask why I seemed upset. The next day, the boy's "girlfriend" slammed my face into a metal locker as the kids all stood by laughing. A few weeks later, he and another boy held my arms behind my back while the girl and her friend punched me repeatedly, poured water on my new rabbit fur jacket, and pushed my face into the dirty, hard snow. This bullying continued for the remainder of middle school, and I *hated* being me. Eventually, the other girls caught up with me physically, but by that time, my insecurities were deep, and I never found a way to outrun them.

If I felt okay with the world, I allowed myself to look good and be seen. If I wanted to hide, I would intentionally over-eat and gain weight because no one noticed a fat girl. It was my way of either projecting perfection or isolating from fear, neither of which was a healthy approach to living. Since those two extremes were all I knew, I never learned to drive down the middle of the road, in the balanced lane of adolescence and adulthood. Like any race against oneself, crashes occur, and when they did, I would repeat the same mistakes and patterns because I never acquired new coping skills.

My family seemed oblivious to the simultaneous love and anger I felt toward them. As a result, I grew into a frighteningly insecure woman who believed anything I loved too much would eventually hurt me. The birth of my daughter many years later brought me both profound joy and incredible fear. In retrospect, there were times I experienced deep-seated anxiety and emotionally disengaged to protect myself. But, disengaging isn't always an effective way of protecting oneself, especially when there are children involved.

When it came time to model appropriate behaviors and the value of self-love, the messages I sent to my daughter were unhealthy because I didn't know what healthy messages looked like. She watched my actions long before the anger and fighting began. She learned my modus operandi, observed my tendencies, and listened to my negative self-talk. Before she became my accidental victim, she tried to be my greatest cheerleader, to no avail. No child should bear that kind of emotional responsibility. With the wounds of my past and low self-esteem firmly entrenched, it was anyone's guess how a given day would unfold.

It was only later, as an older adult, in therapy, that I finally learned how to release the guilt, shame, and anger I had lugged around for decades. I had grown up viewing the world through a lens of everything "bad" being my fault. As irrational as that may sound, this fueled my insecurities, fears, and projections, especially related to becoming a mother.

We must establish better ways of dealing with our patterns, pain, and triggers before sharing them.

It's frightening to think about, but the following visualization helps to make the point: If you emit exhaust like a car and remain trapped in your inner world with toxic emotional fumes billowing, you will suffer and so will everyone around you. Lack of fresh air and perspective make that space the most *unsafe* place to be.

My childhood family had been breathing poisonous fumes for generations, cracking a window here and there for relief. We were part of a generation raised to believe in loyalty to the family connection at any cost. Today's adult children, however, once they are old enough to understand the harm caused by the toxic environment around them, will do whatever is necessary—they'll even smash the glass out of the proverbial window frames—to let fresh air in. They value their need for self-preservation and healing more than they value maintaining ties to unhealthy parents and harmful patterns of the past, and rightfully so.

This choice to disengage—often appearing as an abrupt action—can leave us, the parents, feeling shattered, lost, maybe even victimized again. When this disengaging occurs, to understand our children's choices, we must stop and look objectively at the options our adult children had in their youth. Were we approachable to discuss these patterns of toxic behavior while they were occurring? Could we have seen and understood life from their perspective? Are we *now* capable of putting our egos aside to make room for the possibility that our way may not have been the best? If we are courageous enough to let ourselves address these questions, we also must be willing to take a step back and think. Maybe we *did* provide some good things, but if your adult child isn't speaking to you or maintains distance, you must ask yourself why. Your relationship depends on it.

To be clear, I am not referring to adult children who didn't like having boundaries and rules enforced in a firm but respectful way, and just decided to not deal with any differences in points of view. I am talking about the families where screaming, yelling, hitting, disengagement, emotional instability, depression, role reversal, addictions, or even worse forms of abuse occurred regularly. Or homes where children escaped daily into their imaginations for relief, support, and a sense of being heard and valued. There's a big difference between feeling valued and being spoiled with things that replace healthy parental engagement.

I know plenty of now-adult children who had few material things yet acknowledge their parents for doing the best they could and creating a loving environment. They managed to parent the right way. I also know families where overreactions, tempers, and strained relationships were the norm, and the children look back and say, "That's the way they were, and I will do better." But some don't. Those parents who unconsciously repeat the harmful patterns of their past do so to their continued detriment and that of their children. It's like straightening the deck chairs on the Titanic, pure futility.

My daughter, and others in her generation, appear to have found a life-boat, leaving behind whoever chose to stay aboard the sinking ship. These "emotional refugees" somehow find and support each other and commit to ending the pain of broken love. Numerous books, articles, and support groups focus on the topic, and they are finding a receptive audience.

I regularly meet other people who have either experienced estrangement themselves or know someone who has. I have spoken to several psychiatrists and therapists who specialize in working with adult children to help them successfully break from their toxic family or specific family member. I hear about it almost everywhere I go. This new generation seems to be focused on learning to understand themselves, ensuring that what happened to them doesn't happen to their kids, hopefully eradicating the possibility of passing down emotionally unstable traits.

They don't just treat their trauma; they want to prevent themselves from repeating it with their own children.

They have found their voices and will not willingly surrender to a generational belief that parents are to be respected no matter what. They have made the choice to move hard and fast, break the cycle, and forge ahead in healthier ways. Could there be a different way to handle this rather than choosing total estrangement? Yes, and I think and hope those who need to do so will eventually find a gentler approach to address these issues when they arise. Nevertheless, I believe humankind will benefit from the choice to dismantle unhealthy family systems.

It's an imperfect solution, as has been true for every generation before this. They may lack in areas that we are more accomplished in, but they are fighting for the chance to live safer, healthier lives. My daughter is in the same state of self-preservation as I was when I was trying to raise her. I can't say she is wrong for choosing to do what she did.

Not all parents will repeat the past's destructive patterns, but many will pass on some type of blind thinking with minimal questioning.

It reminds me of the story about the family recipe for making a ham. The first instruction was to cut both ends off before putting it into the pan. Each generation followed the directions until one woman wondered why the ends were wasted. Not knowing the answer, she called her mom, who didn't know the reason either. They checked it out with Nana, who said her pan was too small. This story may be a silly example, but unconscious beliefs, good or bad, can be passed on to children with little thought about the long-term effects. Many of us don't realize we harbor resentment or buried emotional disturbances from our past as we make decisions, give advice, and display behaviors.

Unfortunately, my blind spots were terrible, and it took a large chunk of my adult life and severe casualties to open my eyes to the "new truth." My personal excavation process left me with a vivid picture as I connected the dots of my past. At the same time, estrangement from my child is an excruciating experience to go through, and yet as a result I have been able grow and finally see the world through a lens of clarity, once and for all. While I can't claim a life full of joy, I move toward acceptance, permitting myself to grieve, and holding myself accountable to keep hope alive in my heart.

CHAPTER 7

Now You See Me, Now You Don't

When we harbor trauma, it may be suppressed and stay dormant, but we don't know what could trigger it. Some people appear to get through life unscathed, but for others like me it's a ticking bomb underneath the surface. Instead of doing things differently in my adult years, I repeated the patterns I had learned from my mother. The thing is, in my mind, I was nowhere *near* as bad as she was, but the yardstick I used to measure myself against was utterly skewed.

My behavior was erratic, self-centered, moody, and charged with anger. I was not an emotionally healthy person. I understand now, far too late, that my mother's death, combined with the intense responsibility I felt for my daughter, triggered the old habits of shutting down, disconnecting, and raging with self-loathing and anger. It spilled out all around me, leaving a wake of toxic fumes behind. My child breathed this scent day in and day out with no way of escaping my misdirected, confused state of mind.

Some of us repeat what we don't repair.

The weeks and months following my father's death were excruciating. I felt responsible for it; I was angry, isolated from friends, and sought what I now know was a sense of control. My mother continued to decline, getting more reactive to insignificant things, such as when I didn't clean my room, and she took everything from my closets, drawers, desk, and dresser and put them in a huge pile on the floor. There was hardly any room to move and I was not allowed out until every last item was either put away neatly or disposed of.

My already anxious demeanor became worse, anchored in remorse, regret, fear, and repressed rage. To this day, I can't recall more than scant details from the years immediately following my father's death. I don't remember if we went away, celebrated holidays, or if I attended school for that matter. In hindsight, l felt like I was in a constant state of self-preservation. I was skittish and felt so unsafe in general that limitations began to feel *good* to me. If I didn't stretch too much or go too far, everything would be okay. I learned early on to push the pain away and get on with life. I bet my daughter might say she felt the same way living with me.

My home's craziness continued, with outbursts and threats from one brother, continued harshness from another, and the increasing level of upset inside me. In between those traumatic moments were enough tender spots to keep me affectionate, hopeful, and loving. It was a strange and lethal combination. My moods swung up and down, my anger mounted, and the more I acted out, the harsher my punishments were. When futility washed over me, I would retreat to my room for hours to write and get things off my chest. My mind became over-active; I started sleeping poorly and found solace in food. The happy-go-lucky girl had disappeared, and I had no idea where to find her.

Clearly, the signs of trauma and emotional instability were present, but no one was capable of recognizing my symptoms as they were likely dealing with their own issues.

Occasionally, I would wash my mother's back as she sat in her bathtub. As weird as that may sound, it was when we talked, and she was calm and relaxed. One night, she asked me how I would feel if she were to marry again. I wasn't thrilled, but I wanted her to be happy. She was still young, and as the warm water ran over my hands, I thought about the possibilities. I had hope for a happy ending for all of us. She eventually *did* remarry, and he was a friend of the family who seemed nice enough. Reality soon set in.

Rude, self-centered, and overbearing, this new "step-dad" often started arguments between my mother and me. His kids were mean and spoiled, but he had a lot of money and frequently threw me a $20 bill for no reason, so I learned to tolerate him. What ensued was a year of more fighting, madness, and jealousy, ending in a hostile breakup. It was all still such a mess. I ran into him with another woman while he was still married to my mom. She was fit, younger than my mother, and glared at me while I screamed at the top of my lungs. I took the sandal off my foot and threw it at him, daring him to utter one word. I wanted to beat him after all the bullshit I had put up with.

The whole experience solidified my belief that loving someone equaled getting hurt. Something happened to my mother after they split up, and she never dated again. I started spending weekends at home because I didn't want to leave her alone. As the years went on, she and I still fought, but I continued trying to please her.

I didn't know it then, but we'd formed a codependent relationship. I could not identify or communicate my feelings and valued pleasing her above caring for myself. Over time, this eroded my trust in myself, my judgment, and my belief that I was capable of functioning outside of my relationship with my mom. I needed her and she had a need to be needed.

By this time, I was entering high school, gave zero fucks about it or myself, and hardly attended. I don't know how I didn't get expelled with the number of absences on my transcript. By the time senior year came, my name was on a list of students not graduating because I hadn't satisfied the state gym requirement. Gym? Seriously? I stayed after school for two weeks and did every dash, pull-up, and hang I could muster to have an actual diploma inside the faux-leather folio they handed out at the ceremony. I believe the teachers pushed me through because they liked me, or maybe they felt sorry for me. I didn't know or care; I left high school and never looked back.

That's when the dreams started: I'd be at school standing in the building called "The Commons," with its stark black-and-white floor. The kids milling around me disappeared into thin air, and I was left alone, staring at the library entrance. I would hear him call my name, so I'd turn around, and there was my father, standing in front of me with arms outstretched as if for me to run and hug him. I wanted to so badly but was always afraid because I thought it meant he was coming for me and that I would have to leave my mother. So, I would stand there and cry, *not knowing what to do*. I had that dream repeatedly for years, often waking to a tear-soaked pillow. Eventually, I stopped dreaming of him, but the feeling of "not knowing what to do" followed me into adulthood, wreaking major havoc in my life.

I was always smart, but we never spoke about college or a career. It was assumed that I would get married and have babies. Ironically, my mother was successful in real estate and ran a small business she had bought with the boys in mind, yet she never encouraged me to do the same. Some of the kids I knew from school were going to college, but most of my close friends didn't plan to go. It was the middle of my senior year when I finally asked why none of the kids in our family went to college. She said, "If you want to go, you can," as if it was a visit to the mall. Psychology interested me, but she promptly dismissed it as a "wasted degree." So, I agreed to major in business, but I had a shitty transcript, and I knew we didn't have the money. The only available option was the community college, and I went for six months.

I also worked two jobs, and making money quickly became a priority for me. I felt like a loser, not going away to a "real" college, and my heart was never in it. So, I dropped out, avoided telling her for a few weeks, and spent the next few years bouncing around different full-time jobs. During this time, I also found my first love, a dyslexic, troubled, and moody "bad boy."

After my graduation, we stayed together until his drinking got so out of control that I had to break away. I loved and wanted to fix him, but he didn't want to help himself. Eventually, my nagging drove him away for good; he cheated with a girl who partied like him, and I was crushed. I started to date much older boys, some of whom I didn't even find physically attractive. My insecurities were so deep; I began to cover them up with people who felt safe. But mom would have no part of the boyfriends I chose, repeatedly telling me that I deserved "better," but her words didn't sink in. I had long-believed I didn't deserve all that much, and I never saw the pattern of selecting poor partners as a manifestation of that belief.

I focused an enormous amount of attention on my clothing, shoes, handbags, makeup, and the pursuit of outward perfection. *If things looked good on the outside, everything would be okay.* This obsession with my looks and outward appearance began to overtake my life, and my habit of spending money got out of control. During one particularly memorable shopping spree, I was not even conscious of what I was spending, only that it somehow soothed me temporarily. After receiving the massive credit card statement from that event, I returned the bulk of my purchases to the store. That should have been a big red flag, but it barely registered. Shopping was only the first of my excessive tendencies, ranging from exercise, eating, religion, cleaning, and pursuit of perfection. Perfection can't be criticized, and critical people can't get hurt because they push others away to avoid closeness. Whatever the focus of my excess energy was, I became overzealous.

I would work out for hours a day or clean to the degree where my son still jokes about how perfect my vacuum track lines were. I now wince at such reminders of that obsessive behavior. Growing up I would get yelled at for walking on mom's freshly vacuumed rugs, to which I would suggest a jetpack so I could hover around to get what I needed. Yet I exhibited the same compulsion and regarded my house more like a museum than a home. I also inherited her strong work ethic. I easily handled multiple jobs, and saved up enough money to comfortably afford a new sports car by age 19!

My dog still loved to ride in the car, so I promised she would be my first passenger. She was 18 years old and partially blind, seeing just enough to run after a brightly colored ball when I threw it across the grass. When I pulled up in my new ride, I was so excited! I took the T-tops off the car and went inside to get my pup. I looked everywhere but couldn't find her. When I questioned my mother, she told me she let her outside and that she must have wandered off.

My excitement over the car was quickly replaced with irritation that she left her unattended. We had an inground pool in the yard with a floating cover on it to trap heat. There was no fence around it, so I never let her out alone and promptly went to find her. I called repeatedly, but she never came. As I made my way over to the pool, my heart filled with dread. There was the blurry outline of my sweet girl floating in the corner, trapped underneath the plastic. I screamed so loudly that my next-door neighbor bolted into the yard. I was holding her soaked, lifeless body in my arms and sobbing uncontrollably. Mom ran out, too, admitting that she called for her and was afraid something might have happened when she didn't return, so she waited for me to come home.

My rage toward my mother was undeniable. I could see the scratch marks on the tiles, depicting a struggle to get out. It was an image that haunted me for many years. She was my best friend, and I let her down. I was shocked, devastated, and didn't speak to or look at my mother for weeks. I never set foot in that pool again, and eventually we moved. It was the first time I viewed my mother as weak; I had always previously thought her to be strong. I knew that I had to find a way to reconcile with her and not let my anger continue to bubble up to the surface. The event represented yet another moment of my life that was handled so carelessly. Another time where I had to just "get on with life," with no allowance for grief, anger, or time to heal. The next week my mother brought home a puppy. I was in a state of disbelief, and although she meant no harm, it was precisely what I didn't need or want. The only solution I could turn to was what I was trained to do, stuff my emotions down.

As I got older, I did the best I could to keep my relationship with my mother as sound and peaceful as I could. We had stopped fighting for the most part, and although she would still piss me off, she was starting to mellow, and I let a lot go. I knew she loved and needed me, and I needed and loved her too. The selfishness of her actions was not something I realized until much later in life. I may not have recognized it then, *but I absorbed it right into my DNA.* Years later, I would be at the helm of my dysfunction and selfishness with my own daughter when I was caught smack in the middle of the chaos I created.

CHAPTER 8

Cool Comfort

Children raised in confusing and unstable environments may be at risk for repeating the pattern well into adulthood. They may choose toxic partners, friends, bosses, or become poisonous partners and parents themselves. Even if they manage to break the cycle with their parenting model, they can still be susceptible to people-pleasing, choosing environments that don't support them, and being easily exploited. Psychiatrist and traumatic stress expert Dr. Bessel van der Kolk says, "Negative childhood experiences can set our brains to constantly feel danger and fear."[iii] Children's brains can be literally "shaped" by traumatic experiences that can lead to anger and emotional issues in adulthood.

Harboring trauma is a risk where the stakes are high and, if triggered, rarely produces a win/win dynamic in life. Behaviors needn't be as bad as mine to negatively impact those around you. It's why sharing my story with those on a similar trajectory is so vital.

As a young adult woman, I was still living at home, working for a small printing broker, and making enough money to have a sense of independence. One night I had to drop off supplies at an account for my mother's business. It was a financial services company, and people there were dressed in suits, skirts, and heels, and it smelled like success. Up to that point, I had six months of college and a smattering of administrative experience. Walking into that office was like entering another world, and I desired it more than anything I had ever wanted before. I asked for the hiring manager's name and number and called to the point of harassment to get a meeting. A college degree was required, but I wouldn't relent, so she finally interviewed and hired me as a receptionist.

Some openings for Registered Sales Assistants were available, and I wanted to apply. I bought my own materials, studied for a month every spare moment I had, and then attended a one-week crash course in the city, using vacation time to take my Series 7. Amid the sneers of some brokers who ridiculed me for thinking I could absorb the material so quickly, I passed with a 97 out of 100.

In the years that followed, I was hand-picked for better positions because my reputation was solid, and I worked for one of the firm's top producers. This experience taught me the relentless pursuit of what you want would yield fruit. When you don't give up, things happen. The problem occurs when we push for the *wrong* things, as I did many times over.

I had been in a serious relationship for a year, and got engaged. My fiancé wanted to pursue a life and career out of state. After we wed, I agreed to quit the job I loved and move. I wanted to let him go without me, get his feet on the ground to be sure it would all work out, and *then* leave if it seemed right. But mom reminded me that I knew his intentions and belonged with my husband. So, I worked with a nasty woman for less money and had over an hour commute each way. My husband never found full-time work, and by the time the first snow fell, we had burned through savings, and I felt cold physically and emotionally. We *both* lacked the tools needed for communication, compounded by me moving away from my family, friends, job, and identity.

I also knew that my oldest brother was living with my mother, and during one of my last visits, I'd seen bruises on her neck. She had kicked him out and put a restraining order on him, but eventually, he made his way back. It simmered in the back of my mind and added to the stress I already felt. As screwed up as my family was, it was my comfort zone, and the quick departure from them was a struggle for me. It was the start of resentment building in a young marriage. I was relieved when we decided to move back home.

We did our best to get reestablished with our tails between our legs, but I never found anyone I liked working with. My self-esteem, already weak, began to plummet, living in the shadow of my husband's accomplishments and career. He once said I was a "AAA ball-player playing AA ball." Although he didn't mean harm, the words pierced me. Never an equal contributor financially or formally educated, I created the narrative that he saved me, and I didn't deserve it, further exacerbating my insecurities. Maybe if had we addressed these issues with counseling back then, things could have improved. Although his behaviors were far less destructive than mine, he had a habit of letting things slide rather than confronting them. Raised in an environment where ignoring things made them go away, his passiveness often fueled my frustration. It was two ignorant viewpoints coming together with no skillset to address them.

Not knowing how to get things on track with our marriage, I thought a baby would help us join forces and align. Everything up to this point was his: the home, the cars, even our friends, and I allowed it to be that way. I was the damsel in distress and he was the Knight with little interest in my limited world. He wasn't a bad guy; we just weren't equipped to handle discord well. My overreactions drove him emotionally further away, his pulling away fueled my insecurities, and the dance became an off-sync, troubling one. Still, we decided to have a baby, and our beautiful daughter arrived eight weeks early, full of attitude, and born into a marriage full of strife and financial ups and downs.

Colicky and prone to extreme periods of screaming, vomiting, and minimal sleep, things were stressful. Neither she nor I slept through the night until she was over two years old. I was tired and rarely deviated from the schedule that comforted her, which meant I hardly ventured out. Being a homebody was less taxing than assimilating into the norm with a screaming child. I see now so much was neither my fault nor hers, but simply circumstance in the early years. It was the perfect storm.

During my first years of motherhood, Mom and I spent nearly every day together with the baby. We laughed and got so much joy from her; I couldn't recall a time when I felt so loved and purposeful. My daughter was bright, moody, and challenging at times, but I didn't care. My husband traveled, worked, and golfed a lot, and my mother became my only friend and confidante. "The Three Amigas" were inseparable, and the pain of the past was a distant memory for me. I didn't recognize the isolated existence I grew accustomed to. I felt happy. My daughter became the center of my universe, and my husband's family couldn't understand it, often commenting about how fixated I was. I expected they would celebrate their first grandchild the way I had seen my family and others celebrate their grandchildren. This didn't happen, and it set me up for constant disappointment and misunderstanding.

When we enter situations with our preconceived notion of what they should be like, we kill the joy and diminish the experience.

One night at a family dinner, I rattled on as I usually did about my daughter's recent accomplishments. My career-oriented sister-in-law looked up from her plate and pointedly asked if there was "anything else I could possibly discuss." Perplexed and embarrassed, I said I lacked a career like hers to get lost in, to which she quipped that "at least she didn't need a baby to validate her life." It *crushed* me, and I expected my husband to say something to alleviate the awkwardness. He stayed quiet, and I tried to let it go, choking back tears and clearing the dishes from the table.

Scenes like this occurred over the years, and the more they did, the more I began to expect them, perpetuating another vicious cycle. Over time, the build-up of negative encounters spurred on more fights and uncomfortable drives home with my daughter taking it all in. My lack of cohesiveness with my husband was more evident than ever, and from time to time, I would weep at the foot of my mother's bed, saying we had no real love at home and that I didn't know what to do. Her response was always the same. "What do you think you will ever do? You have a child, and you need to go home to your husband." So, I always did.

On the eve of my daughter's second Christmas, we celebrated with my family, planning to spend Christmas Day with my husband's. Mom didn't feel or look well that night, but I didn't give it much thought. She and my grandmother had plans to go out for dinner together, but Christmas Day morning, my grandmother called to say she was sick and couldn't go. Panicked, I realized this left my mom with nothing to do, so I quickly asked my husband if she could join us that day for dinner at his parents' house, as I didn't want her alone on Christmas Day.

I knew his mother had an illness she was embarrassed about, and the families didn't exactly see eye to eye, yet no one belonged alone on a major holiday. For reasons I never understood or came to terms with, he gave me an emphatic "no." I was shocked and filled with rage, but didn't erupt. Instead, I dressed my daughter, went to visit my mother before dinner, and cried. She said she understood and that it was my place to be with my husband even though I wanted to get take-out and stay with her. Just one week later, on New Year's Day, she told me she had stage four cancer.

I had left her alone for what turned out to be her last Christmas, and I can't imagine what must have gone through her head. Combined with the guilt already inside me, my resentment toward my husband and his family grew exponentially. Her death, just two months later, spurred a major bout of depression, followed by explosive emotions and a total lack of awareness of the path I was about to take. My daughter was a little over two years old at the time. I lived in a constant state of strife, contributing to an environment where fighting was normal, and spotty positive experiences came and went.

My husband ignored my outbursts, and we never spoke about my feelings or conversed much at all. He would talk almost daily to his sister, who had a flourishing career like his, but rarely to me. I clung even more to my role within the home, yet simultaneously resented the isolating feel of it. My weight ballooned to pregnancy level as I turned toward emotional eating for comfort, and tried to hide myself behind my self-perceived, less attractive body. I remained either emotionally disconnected or enraged. I was deep in a negative spiral, and although I wanted to pull myself out of it, I just couldn't find a way to make it happen.

Eventually, I sought help, followed by years of working to understand the many unresolved issues I had with my mother from childhood, but it was much too late. By the time I started to make sense of it all, I was divorced, making terrible life choices, my daughter was a teen, and our toxic dynamic was well established. In retrospect, I see the alarming behaviors that both of us exhibited. As a screwed-up adult, I couldn't help her through what must have been a debilitating, frightening, and confusing time. As her primary caregiver, I was her source of both love and pain. These conflicting emotions helped her develop into an anxious girl who used many of the same tools I did to self-soothe, such as food, isolation, detachment, defiance, and an overall negative default setting.

I also wasted years blaming my husband for not getting in my face or trying to help me until I took accountability in therapy. I learned to understand his tools and patterns. He did what he was taught to do: keep the peace. He knew it wasn't enjoyable or even reasonable by any standards, but he wasn't equipped to deal with the degree of turmoil and confusion trapped inside me. Nor was it his responsibility to fix me. There is no right or wrong. There can be no judgment. There can only be an acceptance that the circumstances were beyond the scope of all parties involved. Could we have all helped one another? Maybe? Yes? Who knows. Ironically, almost fifteen years later, I have great respect for my ex-husband and his family. Still, it can't erase the early years spent trying to desperately fit in or the painful situations I navigated.

CHAPTER 9

Spilt Milk

With my brain so oddly wired, I never stopped going to the mat with my daughter, and life was a constant struggle for us both. Looking back now, I see that she only wanted to please me and have a sense of normalcy and comfort. *These things are a child's birthright.* But my negative expectations, mood swings, and lack of gratitude added to anyone's concerns in approaching me. What an unfair situation to have placed them in. As my behavior escalated, stacking with other destructive ways, my interpersonal connections rapidly deteriorated. As did my ability to center and calm myself long enough to let reason set in. Like a giant snowball rolling down a mountain, I collected more mass and momentum, which continued to work against me. I had no idea what I was dealing with when I was younger, so the habits and behaviors carried well into adulthood.

Understanding this dysregulation piece is vital for getting appropriate help.

It becomes much like a chicken and an egg, where we don't know what comes first. Does the action lead to a reaction, or does a reaction trigger the response? Today, we have more knowledge of why traumatized kids may appear disengaged, prone to depression, anxiety, anger, and why they withdraw or react due to seemingly trivial issues. Sometimes it's not just a kick in the ass that's needed to correct a situation. Once released into adulthood, these people can wreak havoc in their lives and the lives of others. It's much harder to undo damage, repair relationships, or restore other people's lives after they have been negatively impacted than it is to have prevented that negative impact from occurring in the first place. Current treatments and professional help deal with strengthening self-regulation, but recognizing the problem behind the behavior is the first step.

Bad blueprints can destroy families for generations to come.

Mine may be extreme examples, but plenty of emotionally unavailable people leak small doses of poison daily simply because they don't realize it's happening. Children take things to heart. They do dumb things sometimes because they don't know any better. *Adults should know bette*r. Regardless of what happens, we must control our response to it.

I often have tears streaming down my face as I write, think, or try to work through my past, as I do right now. "Spilt milk" is not only an expression used to remind us that things are behind us and that we can do very little to change those events, but also a vivid memory for me. It represents one example of a day and an overall demeanor I am ashamed of and heartily sorry for.

Our daughter was in first grade when she innocently knocked over a glass of milk across the fancy, new, tile kitchen table. It had grooves everywhere, and the liquid ran into every crevice, dripping onto the floor beneath it. I can still recall her shocked face as well as my gross overreaction. We were late for school, and I had an appointment that morning.

I launched into a fit because I had to clean the mess before it dried between the cracks. Seriously, who gives a shit? I apparently did, and this kind of chronic overreaction to such unimportant things ate away at my relationship with my daughter. You'd think I would have realized my meltdown was an inappropriate reaction, but it was normal to me. Many other examples plagued me with guilt once I realized how unnecessary the fights were. I was the careless one, not my daughter.

All I needed to say was: "It's okay. It's only a glass of milk; let's get on our way so we aren't late for school, and I will worry about it later." I didn't have the capacity to respond appropriately, and she suffered as a result. Many scenarios like this occurred over time, and the older my daughter got, the more confused she became. I loved her with every bit of my heart yet chastised her at every turn, fueled by overreaction, aggression, and unjust punishment. For reasons I never understood or stopped to figure out, she became the target of my repressed anger. She had a strong-willed personality like me. Unfortunately, instead of celebrating it, I resisted and resented it, causing her to become defiant.

She learned to equate being loved with being hurt, criticized, and feeling unheard.

Growing up in my family, my eldest brother was very awkward at the table, often spilling multiple glasses of water, wine, and coffee, even as an adult. I remember my mother's overreaction to it and just about everything else he did. He grew up to be a very troubled adult, with a lot of anger and distance from the family, and he never got himself the help I genuinely believe he needed. The stress and fighting in the home from the time he was a small child clearly impacted him. That same atmosphere taught me how to interact with my kids when they made mistakes or disagreed with me. I am not saying this to blame our parents for everything, but I am suggesting that we may take on traits that were modeled for us, and unwittingly impact other people in the process.

CHAPTER 10

Where There Is One

I had the opportunity to break old patterns of behavior and propel two healthy adults into this world to make their mark. Instead, I chose to run a screwed-up relay race, handing off broken batons to my two most cherished people, my children. As a parent, I often think that they succeeded despite me, not because of me. This wasn't the legacy I ever thought I'd leave, and living with it is something I must deal with every day.

In fairness to those who struggle with *any* disorder, there must be an understanding that they needed help. In my case, and the case of my family, we could not see the many red flags at the time. In other cases—and this was also true for me—someone can be dealing with multiple issues, creating a perfect storm of conflict and confusion. I don't use this as an excuse for past behavior, but to experience some quiet within my soul, to keep healing and embracing the new me.

I wonder how often people slip into poor mental health within their homes and families, either undetected or ignored, to keep the peace or walk the path of least resistance. Mine was an extreme case, but most extremes start somewhere slower and quieter. Extremes grow and manifest over time as habitual actions become better tolerated. Once I was able to soften my stance by viewing myself and others through a lens of compassion, I finally found the capacity to forgive myself and interact with others from a softer, healthier place. You can do the same.

The internal fight can be a personal hell, and even once addressed, can be tormenting without forgiveness.

I kept trying to fix my childhood and make things "right" by choosing similar (toxic) situations and people, yet expecting different outcomes. It was completely impossible, but I was too young and self-centered even to grasp that concept, so I plodded along, trying to figure out why I could never be happy. I was always looking for *more*. Drop that dreaded word from your vocabulary right now if you want to experience true inner peace. More is a relative term and leads us onto the trap of the hedonic treadmill of life. We acclimate to constantly seeking and acquiring more, and with each new "success" we experience less satisfaction. Ironically, I now live a life filled with much less, and everything I do experience is much more meaningful.

I did my best to engage in life, almost by proxy, and the years sped by. There was so much hostility at home that our daughter was used to it. It became her "normal," too. I would yell, and her dad would ignore me. He would ignore me, and I would get louder. Sound familiar? If so, I urge you to look closely at the relationship and deal with the environment. The dance we danced was one of the missteps and poor footing we had ignorantly embraced, and neither of us had the skills needed to help the other.

Yet, somewhere in this mix, he said that we owed my daughter a sibling and that being an only child was not good for her. His motto was "Where there is one, there ought to be two." Just like that, amid the madness, our son was conceived. By the time he was born, things had settled down from a war zone to a non-event. We cohabitated in a disconnected, run-the-business-of-a-family sort of way. My spouse felt like an ATM, and I felt like a piece of furniture. Neither of us knew what to do, so we did nothing.

In addition to raising the kids, I had the small business that my mother had started and I took over after her death. It kept my mind busy, generated extra income, and was a chance to create something for myself. An opportunity came along for me to grow it in a significant way. Although riddled with self-doubt, I put together a spreadsheet that calculated all necessary costs and presented it to my husband. Excited and scared, I knew there was no guarantee I'd get the business, but it allowed me to *try*. He quickly dismissed it, saying we didn't need more moving parts than we already had. I felt deflated but assumed he always knew best.

Years later, my biggest client filed for bankruptcy, taking all my surplus cash. It was the beginning of the end for my little business, and a piece of me died right along with it. I had a few other creative ideas in the early years of marriage, such as a greeting card line and my pottery painting store, long before either became popular. My suggestions were always squelched by my husband for being too much of a nuisance to try. I attached feeling worthless to anything other than keeping a home and raising children, yet I felt like a failure at both.

Isolated, and with no close friends or suitable outlets like therapy or activities to keep me feeling productive and healthy, I slipped into apathy and a state of self-pity. Years went by, and no matter how much food I ate, clothing I bought, errands I ran, or holidays I hosted, I couldn't satisfy my need for validation. I *thought* I needed my husband's approval, but what I really needed was my own. In the absence of external validation, I stewed in my warped interpretation. You'd think that at some point someone would have said, "I think you need help, you are depressed and lashing out in anger inappropriately," but no one ever did, and I wonder if I would have heard them anyway. I use the analogy that if I were a diabetic, I would need insulin. If I had an addiction to pills or alcohol, someone might have tried to intervene to get me help for the sake of the family, even if not for me. But it didn't happen, because I had no external support network and I couldn't see it myself. Someone recently told me, "You can't see the picture from inside the frame," and it's true.

I won't allow myself to use this as an excuse anymore, though. Excuses prevent us from accepting accountability and pursuing the healing we need. Somewhere along the line, I feel should have been able to stop my own madness or at least acknowledge it, and seek help. It's as if someone else replaced me when I flew off the handle, and I didn't recognize her. Often, I wouldn't remember a thing. Eventually, I'd calm down and do my best to apologize, but it was always too late. The awkwardness eventually drove friends or family away, and no one knew which version of me would show up, not even me.

CHAPTER 11

Order In The Court

The next thing I knew, my children were school-aged, and I had wandered into the realm of faith. I had found the Lord, though I was the only person in my entire family to do so, which added to the growing tension and disparity. Over-zealous but harmless, I turned to Jesus to steep myself in healing. At first, I seemed to have found a reason to stay grounded in prayer and community, but it was short-lived. Unfortunately, my relationship with my daughter was full of strife. Had I opened my eyes, *my spiritual eyes*, I would have seen that she was just a kid, torn and confused, like I was. Maybe all she needed was a real presence, but I didn't know how to be there. Her brother was usually easy-going, creating a disparity between the two. Their dad, busy with work and not wanting to hear me bitching or them complaining, would often allow them to not listen to me to keep the peace. This taught them behaviors that stem from a disunified front and triggered more reactions in me. There was not much warmth or outward affection for them to see, and they had no example of how fulfilling relationships can be when done well.

For several years, I prayed relentlessly, committing my marriage and family to God, refusing to give up my footing. Over time, though, my faith began to wane, along with my determination to keep things together. I drew away from the church, isolated, left to my thoughts on reality, not God's. For me, this was disastrous. Incapable of seeing any hope or something positive to cling to, I sank into a sadness that began to overtake me. I was surrounded by many blessings but had fallen into such a dark place that I couldn't see them.

One day, I came back from putting the kids on the bus and sat on the bench in my front yard. I cried uncontrollably, and in the space of what seemed like minutes, hours had passed. I couldn't take another day, night, or minute in my skin, yet I didn't know what to do. We all fought terribly that night, and I felt confused and disconnected. I reverted to the only thing I knew how to do—*run away*. The big-girl version meant divorce.

While crying on the bench, I didn't understand that I wanted to escape from what I thought was the *outward* cause of my pain. In reality, the person I was running from was *me*. My brain was a train off the track again. Between my skewed late 30s thinking, and my self-serving ten-year-old in the driver's seat, we drove my life right off the proverbial cliff. I continued to search for external ways of satisfying an inner deficit. *Nothing is capable of filling the inner-vacuum created by trauma or mental illness.* Like a wardrobe, some people wear it better than others, but the hole must become whole at the end of the day. I hadn't a clue, and down the rabbit hole of single parenting and self-imposed stress I went.

Unfortunately, we follow ourselves everywhere.

We sold our house, and I bought something I couldn't afford on my own. My heart was in the right place, knowing my kids liked it and would be safe. Between alimony, child support, and working full-time, I just about made ends meet, but not quite. Not smart. The kids shuffled back and forth, primarily living with me. I was scared, emotionally drained, and most of my family blamed me for my choices. They weren't wrong. The inner vacancy I sought to fill made me vulnerable to inferior choices and set me on neither a better nor more fulfilling path, but ultimately emptier than when I had begun. Worse yet, my kid's lives were changed forever. My son went into aftercare, and I was often tired and stressed out. I ran on fumes, trying desperately to accommodate working, parenting, dating, and family obligations. My daughter became resentful, and the fallout of the swift change became apparent. I blew many things up during that time, but my daughter was to become by far the biggest casualty.

I eventually learned the hard way that I needed to hit the pause button and find out the "why" behind my choices or I would continue to make poor decisions based on feelings rather than facts. I set out on a path of self-discovery, rebuilding, and forgiveness. I had gone into survival mode and shut almost everyone out of my life. I got into therapy and made a list of all the people I had either hurt or abandoned.

One by one, I called each person, forgiving each for whatever they did and asking for their forgiveness. I didn't realize without the capacity for self-love and self-forgiveness, the external love could never sink in. Unbelievably, at the top of that list was my oldest brother. Over a decade had passed since I had seen or heard from him.

CHAPTER 12

Cold Calling

It was mid-January when I made that first call to my brother. The silence was deafening as I said, "Hello," and the awkwardness of the moment made my stomach turn.

I quickly blurted out that he could hang up if he wanted, and I would understand, but I wanted to say, "I love you." He stayed on the line and spoke to my pre-teen daughter for the first time. We spent hours on the phone that afternoon and spoke every few days. A little later in the month, my other brother hosted a family gathering at his home, and our oldest brother showed up. Barely recognizable, years of drinking and health issues had turned this once potent, angry, dominant force into a feeble, frail man. I had spent most of my life fearing him for his violent temper, but I suddenly pitied him, and my remorse was terrible.

We began again that day, talking regularly and laughing over dumb things. I remembered his wit, humor, and poetic brilliance. He had traveled the world on a shoestring budget, started and stopped many careers, and blown up his own life early on, too. He had a great-paying job in his late twenties, owned a home, and was engaged to a terrific girl. Eventually, she broke it off because of his volatile temperament. He couldn't figure out a way to not let his emotions get the best of him, and his life unraveled like a spool of thread.

By mid-February, he had had a severe bleeding stroke and was left in his apartment by his alcoholic girlfriend, who went to work, oblivious to his physical condition. By the time she arrived back home, he was unresponsive but alive, and she called 911. Somehow, they got in touch with my middle brother as next of kin, who promptly notified me.

We all gathered at the hospital. By the time I got there, my other two brothers had given the green light for surgery to save his life, a procedure that led to multiple surgeries, resulting in an induced coma and a grueling recovery ahead for him. He later developed lung cancer, requiring another surgery. With no money or decent benefits, the care he received was sub-par. He bounced around to different hospitals, eventually ending up in a place like nothing I'd ever seen. Lost, forgotten, and hopeless people milled around the chaotic halls, some sneaking out with IVs intact to get drugs. I feared for his health and safety and wouldn't leave him unattended for too long. I felt I owed him.

I worked about forty-five minutes from the city he was in, so two nights per week I would visit while my daughter picked up the pieces at home. On the weekends, I'd spend more time getting him clothing, food, and whatever else he needed. Twice I found him nearly dead from faulty equipment or lack of medicine. Personal items were often stolen from his room, and yet he overcame. Amazingly, his grit pulled him through, he came out of the coma, and I was there when he opened his eyes. He couldn't speak initially, so I would sit near him and let him suck on a lollipop, being careful to hide it from the nurse when she came in.

Eventually, he learned to talk and left a message on my answering machine. Barely audible, I could make out, "Call me." It was like a baby's first words! Soon after, he learned to walk, get dressed, feed himself, and everything was okay, at least for a few months. He was getting short of breath, and an X-ray showed another large mass in his abdomen. He also contracted a horrible bacterial infection, landing him in medical isolation. Unfortunately, I was exposed, got very sick, and couldn't see him for over a month. When I did finally return, he was so sad and lonely. He clung to me like a child, not a sibling, and in that room all our old wounds came out. After almost a year of fighting, he declined rapidly.

We talked about many things the last week of his life, just like I had done with my mother. He asked me to forgive him and thanked me for showing him what love was. After several days in a row of long visits, he knew I was tired and that it was time to let go. I stayed with him, just as with mom, but neither of them passed until I had left. It was almost as if they knew. In retrospect, it was *he* who taught me how to love and God who orchestrated the entire season. It was costly, draining, and taxing on my kids yet again, but in the end, it proved to be the right thing to do and one of my more valuable experiences in life. The eighteen months spent caring for the man who had instilled so much fear and anger in me as a child taught me that forgiveness transcends time, allows peace and even love to grow in place of negative emotions. It was a start, yet I still had far to go.

CHAPTER 13

Sweet Sensations

My post-divorce "freedom" brought a host of feelings, desires, hopes, and visions of a brighter future—a life filled with love, peace, and comfort. The problem with this plan was that there was no way I could attract someone good for me in the absence of healthy *self-love*. I could have taken the quiet, reflective path, fixing and re-defining myself from the inside out. That's what we all needed the most, but it seemed too hard at the time. It was more enticing to get lost in the ups and downs of dating, but it was far too soon. I kept moving so I didn't have to think about anything, and the selfishness of this mindset disturbs me to this day.

My inner scoreboard kept flashing data I didn't want to accept: life 10, me 0. With my self-perception and inner-blueprints so skewed, the worst was far from over. The busier I stayed, the better I felt, so I was always on the run. For a while, things seemed better, dare I say even happier. My kids and I were getting along (at least from my vantage point), so I kept going. I didn't correlate this behavior with the other self-soothing techniques I had used. All different actions, yet similar in the way they filled an inner need, sometimes appearing careless. Like a puppy let loose for the first time, I began dating with great enthusiasm! I told myself I was broad-minded, open-hearted, authentic. In reality, I was very naïve.

I tangled up with a handsome chef and was instantly smitten. Alpha, somewhat narcissistic, and all things passionate, he wrote me love letters, professed his emotions, and soon even my daughter fell in love with him. I recall the day she flopped onto her bed and said, "He is the best thing to ever happen to us," and I heartily agreed. I didn't yet understand my inner "radar lock" on poor partners because I didn't know the appropriate pace, feel, and experience of good relationships. I fell hook, line, and sinker for the "love-bombing," and so did my kids. About a year later, trouble started brewing in paradise. With bad credit, a hard-to-pinpoint past, and some emotional issues of his own, things took a harsh turn. He was often agitated, easily angered, and volatile. The relationship ended when, during an argument, he picked me up and slammed me into a wall, tearing my rotator cuff. I called out of work the next day and went to the doctor. The nurse kept repeatedly asking what happened, but all I could say was that I fell. My tears spoke otherwise, but my tongue would not align with the truth.

At the same time, their father had moved in with a woman my kids didn't like, who sometimes treated them rudely over unimportant things. I remember my daughter calling me in tears one day, and my heart broke. The searing pain and remorse for my choice to move forward with divorce rose to the surface. What had I done? Thinking about it was maddening since there was no way of correcting the situation, and my shame and guilt ate away at me. Both kids deserved so much more. My daughter felt burdened with regulating herself and her brother while doing her best to stabilize her father and me. It was a lose-lose situation for everyone involved, especially for the kids. No matter what I did, I couldn't keep the "body" of my choices from rolling back up to my feet. My carelessness dictated all of our circumstances and outcomes.

I allowed ALL of us to give our hearts away, and just like that, they were broken. My daughter never got close to anyone I dated ever again. My shoulder eventually healed, but a piece of my spirit didn't. My children learned not to trust my judgment and to remain closed off from their parents' partners. I subconsciously committed to "fixing it" with other unhealthy partners in a futile attempt to create a happier ending. My own narcissistic-like traits and comfort around other, critical, narcissistic people ensured that I kept finding them on my radar, like a heat-seeking missile programmed for a mid-air explosion.

Time went by, and eventually, I got back into the dating world. Still bruised deeply inside, not acing Parenting 101, nor coming from a place of confidence and self-love, I continued with what I knew how to do: work feverishly for critical people to please them and validate myself via the affection of others. After the disappointment of a few emotionally unavailable men, I eventually found someone while sifting through endless needles in the online dating haystack. If you want to avoid being present with yourself, dating sites are a great way to do it. I had no idea that the new relationship I was about to jump into would eventually damage my psyche *and* my financial well-being.

When we don't learn the lesson, sometimes the heat gets turned up.

I was supposed to heal my inner-self so that I could attract and identify stable partners and friends. But I refused to look inside and, as a result, created another round of turmoil. There was no time left to string two cohesive thoughts together between working and dating, let alone get to know myself or establish healthy relationship parameters. I dated this new man for several years, with the first year great, and the rest heating up like a pot of water coming to a slow boil. I didn't feel it happening, or maybe, just didn't want to notice. I only saw what I wanted to see. Wash, rinse, repeat.

We would often fight, and resolution came only with me offering the olive branch. My kids learned to keep a certain distance, and, in hindsight, I don't blame them. As per my usual open-book ways, I over-shared everything about myself. My ups, downs, savings, earnings, stories, and the like. No filter, no boundaries, and zero self-awareness. My friends and family never cared for him, with the overarching comment of "We just want you to be happy," leading the way. Eventually, a more critical, demeaning, and selfish side emerged from him, but I had a way of letting it go since it was within my internal mapping. I equated someone being critical of me with loving me, so his treatment of me was well within my "comfort" zone.

I was determined to stick with him and *finally* do something right. But a few years in, he crossed even my major boundaries, and I broke off our relationship. Professing love for me, he came back and asked for a second chance, offering me an unexpected engagement ring. I knew if I said no, I was on my own, and if I said yes, I was lowering my standards by allowing him to get away with what he did to me. Although I didn't have peace with saying yes, I believed that no one else would *ever* love me. So, I accepted the ring. We never set a date, spoke about a wedding, or did anything an average, happy, engaged couple would do. It was odd.

This path of least resistance allowed self-loathing to slowly creep back in. Over time, he began to exploit my wounds, fears, and kindness. My people-pleasing tendency ensured that the cycle continued. Emotionally manipulative and critical traits were also things I possessed, so it *all* felt familiar to me. However, it also exacerbated my lack of self-worth and fueled the flames of already stressed relationships with my adolescent children. My daughter retreated, and my son stayed at arm's length.

Not long after, he needed a place to live and asked if he could stay with me. I had a brief conversation with my son, and just like that, this man moved in. He knew this would cause the loss of my permanent alimony, but assured me that he was my forever guy. Things went downhill quickly. He lost his job, unemployment stopped, and I was struggling to keep things afloat. It was a shit-show, and I was the star.

During this time, my young niece was diagnosed with cancer, and since I had let so many relationships go by the wayside, I wanted to see her every weekend I could. For five months, I allowed every other responsibility to slide outside of work. I started sleeping poorly, and rapidly gained weight. I was riddled with anxiety and fear. My son had two years left in high school, and the real estate bubble had burst, leaving my home worth significantly less than what I owed on my mortgage. I couldn't find a solution to my emotional and financial crisis and worry manifested on my face, body, and health.

CHAPTER 14

The Breaking Point

It took the painful loss of my daughter from my life to grind me to a halt, getting me to this point of accountability and understanding. I share my story here in the hope that you can prevent ever feeling such grief. I encourage you to do what I didn't until it was much too late: *take a step back to reflect on how it is your relationship got here.* These situations grow over time. You both may have a part to play, but someone needs to extend the olive branch and open communication lines while there is still time.

Biological relationships have little to do with emotional attachment.

If you are dealing estrangement from your child, it's crucial to find a professional who can help you get to a place of objectivity and examine your behaviors. When we remove our emotions, we see the facts. You may or may not suffer from an additional underlying issue, but imagine how crucial it can be to get proper support if you *do*.

Regardless, if you have become a trauma trigger for your child, they may feel there is no other solution but to implement hard boundaries around your relationship. It's essential to find a place of understanding from their vantage point, and that is not an easy thing to do. It requires a parent to let go of the belief that "blood is thicker than water" because, at times, it's not. Other adults may have filled the void for your child, becoming surrogate parents for them. Much like adoptive children often feel after finding their birth parents, the one who was there for them every day is considered mom or dad.

If you still have contact with your child, but it's strained, I hope you can open your heart to see that things aren't the way they should be. Let this book spur you on to self-discovery, conversation, and the quest for space and healing so that a hard stop never gets put into place between you and your child. It's a delicate balance, and the only trait that will serve you now is humility. Being right can equate to being lost.

If you find your adult child to be headstrong or incapable of seeing anything "your way" even after years of you "trying," you need to accept that this may never change. It does not mean it's another thing to blame yourself for, but it *does* mean that you must learn to understand the behaviors or remain in discomfort. Decades of a strained interpersonal relationship means patterns are likely to be firmly entrenched. Learning to release the triggers and responses elicited by your adult child gives you the ability to parent in a better way now.

When we cannot fully release ourselves from past wounds, they can continue to negatively impact our lives in the present. Growing up with feelings of low self-esteem, guilt, and codependency, I chose people, jobs, situations, and things that provoked and triggered me in a continued effort to *self-destruct*. It was an unconscious, self-sabotaging cycle from which I did not know how to break free.

My heart was always soft, but I would lash out and inflict pain on those closest to me, select partners that exploited my weakness, and blow up anything that would potentially start to feel good. This revelation took my breath away, along with a good chunk of everything I valued in life. The terrible irony is that I am now empathetic to as many people as I can be, listening and helping them sort out the chaos they feel inside. I remind them that their guilt and remorse maintain a karmic wall between them and the ones they love. Although I now come from a healthier place with a handle on my trauma, I can't "un-ring a bell" or undo the damage that has been done.

For a while, I sent text messages to my daughter from time to time expressing my love, which was probably unfair to her. She might not feel the love back. Each time I didn't receive a response, I would hurt. So why did I continue to do it? I didn't understand it then, but I wanted to *desensitize my need* for a reply. When it first happened, I would cry uncontrollably, checking my phone repeatedly for days. Now, I only experience a lump in my throat, followed by sadness. That's an improvement, if you can call it that, given the situation. *My goal is to send the text and move in love to such a degree that I am entirely detached from the outcome.* She may not need to hear that I love her. It might possibly even anger her. Part of my healing is to accept that love is not always a two-way event. The only way I have of testing my growth is to express how I feel and see what occurs, knowing it will likely be nothing. How do I react in the presence of that absence of data?

I am not advocating that you do the same, as my ways aren't for everyone. I have a deep need to know that someday when my time comes to leave this earth, I don't pine the way my mother did. I want to arrive at a place of knowing I can love my child with nothing in return and be in the presence of the feeling without pain. Is it attainable? I don't know. Take peace in knowing that you don't need to agree, be validated, or understood. Don't take anything personally, and focus on seeing your child through the eyes of love. If boundaries are required, keep them and let them be. Think of it as your opportunity to parent with the patience that once eluded you.

We cannot control how someone interacts with us, but we can change how we respond to them.

The breaking point for me was the year I lost my niece and realized I had created another broken romantic relationship. During this crisis, I leaned heavily on my daughter, yet again, for advice, comfort, and venting. She was away at college but still speaking to me, and often I would call her crying. It was always her responsibility to calm me down, instead of the other way around. How could she ever have come to me with any of her needs, questions, or concerns? I showed zero capacity to handle my own life, with irrational judgment, lacking empathy or understanding. In my mind, it was dialogue; for her it must have been torture. Blind self-absorption, lack of self-regulation, and child-like desperation fueled my every interaction.

One Saturday during my niece's continued decline, I woke up, and my fiancé let me know that he wasn't attracted to me anymore, using the words, "Sickened at the sight of you." My initial reaction was one I'm ashamed to admit: crying and pleading with him to forgive me for letting myself go, promising him that I would try to do better, and didn't want to lose him. That moment was so *low*. I'd never been spoken to that way by a romantic partner before. I had invested years and ruined myself financially for the sake of our relationship, and it had been a disaster, so in my mind, no one else would want to be with me either. I couldn't fathom being alone or start-ing over, so I swallowed my last bit of pride and stayed in the relationship, although it didn't last long.

A few weeks later, someone came across his picture, active on a dating site, and sent me a screenshot. When I confronted him, he went into a fit of rage. I broke the engagement, and when I asked him to leave my home, he refused. For weeks he lived in my basement, stating he had rights, forcing my son and me to live in discomfort and duress with threats he made toward us. Finally, he chose a moving date, and I requested the day off from work to ensure that everything went smoothly. We discussed the ring and agreed that he would sell it to pay me some money and help me out, given my financial situation. He asked me to hang on to it until he had a good deal in hand.

The morning my niece died, I wept for hours and then decided that I would go to work to prepare for a couple of days off to be with my family. Still living in my home, my fiancé heard me crying and came into my room. He hugged me tenderly and told me how sorry he was for my loss and all that had transpired between us. He brought me tissues, hot soup and showed me compassion. As we sat side by side on the edge of my bed, he assured me that everything would be okay. *I believed him.* Somehow, I got myself together, and just as I had done the day after my brother passed, I went to work and remained productive. When I arrived home, before the garage door was even halfway up, I knew something was wrong. I had lots of boxes in anticipation of my eventual move to a less-expensive place, yet they were all gone. I entered the kitchen, and couldn't believe what I saw: stacks of cards given to me by him piled on the counter, and half of everything missing from my cabinets and drawers.

Frantically, I ran upstairs where my TV, cable box, phone, clothing, and personal items were strewn about since the bedroom furniture was gone. I saw the comforter on the floor, and when I picked it up, slash marks ran through it. I immediately ran to where I hid my valuables and cash to find the engagement ring missing. My "Family Emergency Workbook" was open with the usernames and passwords of every account I had. A copy of my Divorce Decree showing my alimony figure circled in bold marker was there for me to see. He intentionally gave me false comfort the day she died, sent me to work, and spontaneously moved out. I couldn't breathe and thought I was going to have a heart attack. I hit redial on the kitchen phone so that a human was on the line with me in case I did. I didn't know or care who it was, and all I could say was "Help."

I didn't die that night, although I felt like I wanted to, and composed myself enough to call a friend to change my locks, my ex-husband to keep my son overnight, and a friend who was a detective to discuss what options I had. Of course, there weren't many. His advice to me was to be glad he moved out and get on with my life since he appeared unstable. He went on to slander and portray me as someone that had taken advantage of *him*. It was an unbelievable and surreal experience that made me question everything I had ever believed about myself.

I was riddled with guilt that my son had to experience this. It solidified my kids' beliefs that I had no handle on my own behavior or life choices.

We buried my niece a few days later, and my daughter didn't attend the funeral. She had her own health issues to battle, so I simply let it go. Looking back, it was another red flag I chose not to see. She was already that disconnected from me. Although I channeled all my grief into work to numb the pain, I found myself in another downward spiral of anxiety, insomnia, anger, resentment, and victimhood. I felt betrayed, abandoned.

A sense of worthlessness pummeled my mind, resurrecting every negative thought and feeling I had long since buried deep. Buried, but not eradicated. I was doing my best to hang on and make it through what seemed like another nightmare that I could not wake from. This experience was enough to send me back to therapy, where I was diagnosed with Post Traumatic

Stress Disorder that lit up when big triggers hit. With the childhood trauma suppressed and left untreated, my patterns of rage and self-loathing behavior throughout the years became clear to me. My misdiagnosis and treatment for only depressive episodes just made my moods harder to control. I had finally found the source.

CHAPTER 15

They Love Me, They Love Me Not

When children suffer from trauma, they sometimes feel they have no "voice" and often hide from the world, attempting to self-soothe and regulate. When these children grow into adulthood, they often dominate conversations, talk out of anxiety or nervousness, and can become self-centered adults. Left unchecked, they can develop narcissistic traits, or worse yet, covert versions of narcissism, being outwardly kind while inflicting control or creating co-dependency. I embodied many of those traits. My daughter also stayed in her own world like I had done as a child, likely attempting to escape or self-soothe from the environment in which she found herself.

Years of my unsettling and victim-like behavior, combined with my desperate and needy tendencies, had taken their toll. The roles were now reversed, and even as I tried to engage differently, I elicited the same responses from her that I used to give. She was mirroring my behaviors back to me. While it is easy to think she was intentionally doing so, I believe it was a case of *her* subconscious trauma surfacing and repeating the behavior patterns she learned from me. This left me perplexed and striving harder because I didn't want to lose her. But desperation repels, and the more anxious and remorseful I became, the more she resented me. It was a no-win, toxic situation. She began to display a visceral reaction to me, just by me showing up.

It reminded me of growing up with the youngest of my three brothers. For whatever reason, he and I always fought. In retrospect, I believe that I reminded him so much of our mother that it was a trigger. As he reacted to me, I responded to him, and it was the same pattern of emotional response and behavior. It was everywhere in my life. I idolized him, but he was usually mean to me, always criticizing my hair, makeup, weight, or clothing. The more I tried to win his affection, the worse our fighting became. He embarrassed and hurt me so badly once that I became filled with rage and tore apart his bedroom. I ripped the poster on his wall, cut the phone line, and threw around some of his things. I was severely punished for my behavior, but no one ever questioned why such a young girl would be so violent or where that level of anger could come from.

He moved out on his own as soon as he could. When I got older, for some reason I developed a need to win his affection. I would visit him, but he was always busy. I usually felt like an intruder, yet I still went. One time he introduced me to his friends at the beach, but didn't mention that I was his sister. When I asked why he wasn't letting anyone know I was family, he pointed to a girl polishing her surfboard and said, "She's my sister." My heart sank, and I wanted to disappear into the hot sand beneath my feet; it was clear that for him, DNA had nothing to do with the strength of a relationship. I was thankful to be headed home later. He was picking up a new vehicle after dropping me at the airport, and as always, I was running late. He was irritated, and by the time I jumped into his truck, it was already running. "If we miss your flight, I am leaving you at the airport," he said. I asked if he could drive faster, but he told me he wouldn't get a speeding ticket because I wasted time putting my "cake-face" on. I was hurt, but he was right, so I shut up.

I was about 15, and by the time we arrived, the flight had departed. We found out the next one was a few hours later and that I could get on it. Then he walked me to the new gate and left. I had no money, and there were no cell phones, so I found an attendant and asked if I could call my mother.

The staff stayed close by, and I got something to eat on the plane, but I never forgot the experience. I stared out the window sobbing the whole way home. *It was another fractured relationship I didn't understand,* and it impacted me well into adulthood. Remarkably, I still visited him after that! It was a cheap, easy getaway for me, but things between us never improved. Eventually, I gave up on the vacations and the relationship altogether.

As a grown woman, seeing him for a holiday or event caused anxiety days ahead of time. We would often disagree, and his harsh nature upset me. I had become just like our mother, so we both were triggers for one another, eliciting the same kind of visceral reactions that occurred between my daughter and me. My internal response to him today is a more normal one. Although I would not call our relationship "close," when I do speak with him or see him now, I feel nothing but love. It took me almost a decade to understand the "why" behind it. When certain personality types trigger a reaction of anxiety or stress in me, I need to remove myself from the situation if I can or find ways to diffuse it when I can't. Seeing others from a place of empathy and understanding taught me to remain centered and grounded and helped me weed out unhealthy relationships, upgrading them for better ones. It also gave me a clearer perspective on my daughter since she struggled with similar challenges when interacting with me. History and patterns repeat if not identified and adequately addressed. I am still actively working to interrupt those patterns wherever I observe them.

Above all, I learned that broken people often hurt others—not always out of malice.

Although the shock of my ex-fiancé moving out unexpectedly was difficult, it paled in comparison when years later my daughter moved out "suddenly" after one of our uglier screaming matches. When she was 17 and in her senior year of high school, she'd had enough of life with me. I came home from work to find her things all gone except for a dusty bookshelf and a few scattered books she no longer wanted. One of the titles was *Living Successfully with Screwed-Up People,* by Elizabeth B. Brown. She had moved to her father's residence in a nearby town, and neither one of them told me about it. I was devastated, but now I realize I couldn't blame her. I sat on the floor of her empty room and just sobbed.

Shortly before she left, we had a massive fight during a phone call where I screamed with rage about being pressured to take on college loans for her that I couldn't afford, and I sounded like an animal. I said things I shouldn't have, including accusing her of an inappropriate sense of entitlement. I had no idea that she was with her father and had the call on speaker phone, so he heard firsthand my out-of-control behavior toward her.

Her father ensured she could commute to finish her senior year of high school and removed her from my house. I had no idea it was coming. I allowed myself to feel betrayed and victimized at the same time—the very patterns that got me into that mess in the first place. But the years prior were the worst for her and me. With my self-induced mounting stress, my ability to regulate steadily diminished, and I became more reactive. Even with multiple attempts with doctors and medicines, nothing worked, and almost everything made me feel worse over time.

She came to visit her brother while I was at work during a terrible ice storm. She fell, shattering her leg while moving her car so the driveway could get plowed. What ensued was hours of surgery, followed by months of being bed-ridden at my place after she had just taken steps to liberate herself from me! I was only six months into a new job and needed two weeks unpaid leave to get her stabilized. The first week after her surgery, I slept in a chair next to her hospital bed as the morphine drip lowered her inhibitions, allowing her true feelings to come out. One nurse refused to come into the room due to her profanities, and I sat sobbing in the hall in disbelief.

I had been the one who asked her to move her vehicle, and although I had no idea the storm was so bad, I regret that decision to this day. The second week, and for months after, she slept next to me in my bed. I set my alarm every four hours to ensure I woke her and kept her as comfortable as possible with pain meds. I washed her each morning, made her breakfast and lunch before I left for work, paid for a woman to check on her mid-day, and was home for dinner. I can't even imagine her resentment about it, but her father felt it was the best place for her until she could walk again. Eventually, she could take limited steps, but had missed half her senior year and went off to college on a motorized scooter. She had many health issues to conquer, and dropping her off in such a vulnerable state was horrific. The fact that she went and succeeded was nothing short of amazing.

She would call from school frustrated and crying. I assured her that her father and I would come and pack her things up, reinforcing that no one would fault her for coming home. As she would calm down, I'd ask, "Do you think you can make it one more night?" Invariably she would say yes. Day by day, she beat the odds and stayed, despite her challenging circumstances. She went on to be a rock-star in college, but kept me at arm's length. I never met her friends, attended awards ceremonies, or became a meaningful part of her life.

In retrospect, whenever I *did* see her, I was usually in the middle of some crisis of my own, so who could blame her? I was on the periphery, and because of my self-centeredness and victim mentality, I could never understand why she wouldn't want to be with me. *It was always about me.* We went through several periods where she pulled away, but she always came back. During holidays or visits, a fight would usually break out, especially if both kids were together, and we were rarely calm or happy. Her childhood wounds were manifesting, but she was determined to get to the root of things far quicker than I could ever dream of having done.

CHAPTER 16

The World's Worst Breakup

The people who love you won't always stay with you if you can't fix your shit quickly enough. This is a hard but true statement to swallow. There WILL be days when despite your best effort to move forward and comfort yourself with assurances that things are not that bad and that self-love and forgiveness are possible, you will still fail miserably. Your heart will rip, and you will experience the re-opening of the wound.

We can lose people to physical death, emotional death, or disinterest—there are all sorts of reasons why people exit our lives. When the one who leaves is someone we want so badly to stay with, the pain of losing them is exquisite. Rather than judge my daughter's actions, I thought about our individual roles in her story and why she felt she needed to take over sole authorship. This was a painful process and took many conversations with young men and women in her situation for me to understand and see things through her eyes. She had a right to heal herself without worrying about my ability to deal or not deal with her choice to move on.

I told myself that she may well have done me a favor, or perhaps had moved as an act of love by saving me from pining uncontrollably at the other end of my phone. I told myself lots of things to keep centered on acceptance, since it was a situation I could not change. I also reminded myself that we shared a common bond, whether or not we lived in close proximity to each other. We were both creating a "new normal." Hers without me, and mine without her. In this way, I was able to view her as moving in the same direction, rather than against me.

If we understand that our estranged ones maintain the authorship rights to their own story, it releases us to move into acceptance.

I won't bullshit you; tears streamed down my face as I typed this chapter. I never said that learning the lesson was easy, but it was necessary. I wouldn't and won't say trite things like "My daughter will regret this someday" or "She will grow out of it and come around" because she may not. Nor will I allow people around me to say similar things to comfort me. I finally learned that that the sooner I accepted the new normal, the better. It sent me on a journey to understand life from her perspective and develop empathy in ways I never had before. I immersed myself in podcasts, forums, and intensive research into neurology and psychology, and encountered other young adult children who had suffered similar wounds from their own mothers.

Although at first it devastated me, it eventually brought me to a place of acceptance. *I had stolen chunks of her childhood, but now that she is separated from me, she can claim her own adulthood, break the patterns of toxic behavior, and learn what healthy, loving boundaries look like.* I love her so much that I want the poison out of her system, even if it means that our relationship will never be a comforting, close one.

Now that I understand what happened in my family, I make it a point to help as many young people and parents as possible to validate their experiences, find healing, and see their parents differently, *if possible.* I don't want to see another parent or child experience life with unaddressed trauma and emotional illness. The way I was raised, parents were who they were, and you stuck with them for better or worse until they passed on. I never heard any apologies for their actions or behaviors. Maybe you can relate to this.

It's a new generation now, though, and these adult children don't believe in blind allegiance to anything or anyone, not even their parents. I have shared my story here to offer a framework of how devastating blind allegiances can be if ignored and passed on. If you were to speak to any of my childhood friends, they would say my upbringing was fine, my mother loved me, and that my family was "funny." They might also tell you stories of being at the diner after midnight when the owner's police scanner blurted out my address, ensuring that I would cut out and head home. To them, it was amusing; to me, it was emotionally draining.

The truth comes in many flavors, and we display the pictures we want to place inside the frame of our lives. As a grown woman, I showed others the image I wanted them to see. I had a beautiful home, marriage, children, stability. One would say we had it all going for us. But did we? I believe we might have if I had taken the proper steps to figure out what drove my underlying behaviors. It can be an exhausting process for ourselves and anyone else involved in our lives when we continue to make changes to outward circumstances, changes which will never address the inward problems. Until we forgive and accept ourselves for who we are—dark parts and all—we are unlikely to align and discover the person we can become.

When this dissonance occurs, we become our own saboteurs, helping others around us while simultaneously blowing up our own lives.

My daughter stayed away, only moving back to the area a few years post-graduation. I was hopeful things could get back on track between us. Unfortunately, they didn't. I was doing hard inner work and changing, but the more I tried to see her, the more she avoided me. I didn't realize it, but she was weaning herself, slowly burying her past, to forge a new life that didn't include me. As her outbursts continued to mount, I noticed my son would rush to my defense, creating tension between them, something I never wanted. Whatever event we were in the middle of would end terribly. For about two years the length of time between visits increased. During this time, months would pass and she wouldn't take my calls, see me for a quick hug, or even let me drop Chinese food at her door. The more I reached out, the worse it became.

Eventually, Spring came, filled with some hope of new beginnings. I made a physical move after a few job changes. I realized that I always chose critical bosses due to past patterns, so I took less money for more peace, started writing on the side, and continued to work on myself. It was like a rebirth of sorts, but trying to fix everything at once was an uphill climb. It also wasn't easy to face having left such a poor "life-scent" behind me. I wanted more than anything to repair things with my daughter. But she wouldn't connect, and I knew in my heart that something had permanently shifted. I continued to check-in via text, get one-word answers, or "I'm busy, sorry" to any request. I always wrote, "Okay, I love you," but never got a response.

One day, almost two years after her return to the area and months after I had last had a quick call with her, my phone rang. I heard my daughter's ringtone from across the room and saw her face flash on my screen. My heart leaped inside of me, and I was so happy that she was calling! The conversation started politely with her asking about my move, but quickly turned into a pointed reason for the call.

I felt a lump in my throat, and I choked back the tears. She had been doing her own inner work, and although she wished me no harm or ill, she felt it best if we parted ways. At twenty-four years old she completed what had a been years of weaning off of her relationship with me. She explained that when I texted or called her, I pulled her out of her new-found peace and happiness, and she felt that we couldn't have a healthy relationship.

I cried, saying how sorry I was and that I wanted to make things right. She said that she needed space and had decided to call me to tell me rather than continue to avoid me. She asked me several times if there was anything else that I needed to say, and even *then*, I didn't realize it would be the last time I would hear her voice. After the call ended, hours passed before I could pick myself up off the bare, wooden floor beneath me. I don't remember the days following the call or how I managed to work, live, or communicate with anyone, but I did somehow. Memories began to flood my mind, many of which I wished I could retract. My bed became the torture chamber where I came face to face with the images of all my words, choices, and actions. I kept her picture beside me, crying night after sleepless night.

After another few months passed, I tried to reach out again. I had read an article written by a young girl who had suffered from terrible PTSD and an abusive relationship with her mother. Her words ripped through my body and I couldn't breathe. I had done the same thing. I finally saw things from my daughter's perspective. I saw that even though I was her "mother," I hadn't fulfilled or earned the title. I had taken everything for granted, especially her. She had strangers in her life who had created more of a nurturing environment than I had. I wrote a long, heartfelt text and told her how much I loved her in a final attempt to communicate. Her reply to me was when a part of me died.

She wrote that the very act of contacting her, continuing to apologize and tell her that I loved her, was proof that I hadn't changed my self-centered ways, as it was to assuage *my* needs and guilt. It wasn't for her benefit, since she had moved on and requested no contact, and you know what? *She was right*. I had never seen it in that light before.

Every time I did anything it was for my benefit, not hers. My apologies meant nothing to her now, as she no longer had any need for them. She had even taken to calling me by my first name, only occasionally referencing me as "mom." Yet, even in the moment, I still couldn't see it as it was happening. I would scroll through her Facebook, liking her posts, or commenting on things as if we were "connected" even when she had me at such a distance; it was merely a matter of time before she felt ready to disengage, and it never occurred to me that she would take that final step. In my desperation, I was willing to take whatever level of relationship I could have with her, never seeking to understand her needs and only seeing what I wanted to see.

She had let me know that she was happy, the healthiest she had ever been, at peace with her choice, and did not want to provide false hope of a reconciliation. She said she had forgiven me, knew I couldn't help myself because of my own trauma and illness, but needed me to understand that I am a constant reminder of all HER trauma, pain, and hurt.

She knew I loved her and asked me to not spiral out of control, but to understand and respect her choice and move forward. I wish I could say that I handled it well, but truthfully, it was the hardest year of my life. I'd get flashes in my mind of things I said and did, and the ensuing waves of guilt, shame, and remorse were too painful to take some days. Truth be told, it still is from time to time. My son, the peacemaker, must feel "stuck" between us. While his relationship with his sister was volatile at times, they still remain close, and I hope that continues.

Although I was making strides in accepting my situation, I experienced major setbacks. One such time was a night my son was coming over for dinner. Early in the day, I changed into a wallet I hadn't used in years. As I put my money into it, I saw folded papers, notes from my then eight-year-old daughter telling me how much she loved me, how great I was, and that everything would be okay. I had forgotten all about them.

The memory of her "trying" brought me to tears. I carefully and lovingly folded them back up and placed them back into the slot. My emotions were on high alert combined with little sleep, and I should have canceled our dinner plans but didn't have the emotional strength. He arrived, and somehow, the topic of Instagram came up. That's when it happened.

His sister had already cut me off from Facebook but must have forgotten about Instagram. I occasionally looked at her page because seeing her pictures was like a shot of oxygen after weeks of not breathing. It gave me a strange peace of mind. In one sense, it heightened my awareness of being out of her life, yet provided a much-needed sense of comfort, seeing her look happy and well. I went to look at her page only to see that she had disconnected there too. I didn't know when you view a person's "story," such as I had done twice the day before, that person can see it. I called attention to the connection, and just like that, it was gone.

I had promised my son I would not cry, engage in discussion about, or reference his sister in any way, but right there in my kitchen, I broke into tears. I felt like Tom Hanks in "Cast Away" as he watched his friend Wilson float away into the ocean. My one last tether had been cut, and it severed my heart. What ensued was an argument and uncomfortable afternoon with my son, despite my efforts to stay composed. He may never understand that moment, and that's okay.

At first, I took it so personally—*the exact response that put me into that situation in the first place.* I was hurt, felt it unnecessary on my daughter's part, and was defensive. Then, I sank into that dark place inside my head for a few days, unable to sleep yet still working with high functionality. It took a two-hour cry in my bathtub to come to the place of realization that it wasn't about me. For my daughter, it was about her! Regardless of why she chose to do it, it was her right to make that choice, not mine. When we struggle to connect with a person and can't, it leads to scrutinizing everything we ever did, which is madness. Being written out of someone's real life script hurts. For actors on a movie set, being written out of a script is just the end of a job, but it's not the end of the world. For the rest of us, though, being cut out of a loved one's life *is* for real, and yet we still try to cling to an ending that *we* want, an ending that makes *us* feel good. The only ending any of us can write is our own, and we have the right to do so, but we cannot control who else will choose to be a part of the chapters of our lives or who will choose to exit.

CHAPTER 17

Facing Triggers

Although I was on a better path of healing, albeit still wrestling with the outcomes of my choices, my daughter's decision to completely sever ties with me was the most significant setback I had yet to encounter. I understood her choice and ultimately agreed that I hadn't earned the right to occupy a spot in her adult life. However, it activated almost every fear and emotion I grapple with: failure as a parent, being alone, lack of worth, imposter syndrome, self-loathing, no family connection, remorse, and fear of death—an event that will push me to face what I believe will be an "accounting" of what I did in my life.

It was not my daughter's action but rather my *response* to her action that triggered a new crisis for me. I have since learned that our feelings—even if they seem valid and factual—can be irrational. While acknowledging our feelings is hugely important, we still must control how we respond to them. Otherwise, we risk fueling them and allowing them to take on exaggerated forms of themselves, wreaking havoc inside our minds. If we don't calm down and let go of the excess energy directed at the downward spiral, we may succumb to rebound behaviors such as binge-eating, gambling, excess shopping, careless sex, drinking, drugs, retreating, or whatever else we do to numb the pain. Each trigger sets off very similar patterns, actions, and responses. It's critical to confront our feelings, acknowledge them, get them out where they can be seen and felt—safely, of course—rather than stuffing them away in hopes of not having to deal with them. When we work through them as soon as they come up, rather than wallow in them beyond a healthy release of emotion, we can avoid wasting precious time spinning in mental circles.

Therapy, meditation, calming rituals, nature, or anything that creates a change in the physiological state can help to mitigate the onset of triggers and the emotional responses we have to them.

There is a distinct difference between me experiencing a depressed state versus the resurgence of trauma. Both make me cry and feel a sense of hopelessness or unworthiness. But the duality of sadness layered with a trauma response requires an entirely different approach to healing. For me, things that numb my pain, like alcohol, anti-depressants, and the like, *delay* my recovery from a depressive episode. It took me many years to realize this. My brain needs to be fully aware to recalibrate, regulate, and come back to center. This is not to say that I am against medications; I feel meds *can* play a helpful role in things like mood stabilization, slowing racing thoughts, easing depression, alleviating anxiety, and mitigating many other disorders that are not always easily identified. The key is to make sure the correct diagnosis is made, and the best treatment options explored, considering the parts and pieces that make up your unique situation.

Often, people with trauma have other underlying disorders. Or perhaps, people with underlying disorders experience exacerbated trauma responses. Either way, they make situations worse and this was certainly true in my case. Most of my life was spent unaware of the factors that contributed to my struggles with various harmful behaviors. Since trauma plays a part, diagnosis and treatment were not clear-cut, and long-term solutions remain a work in progress. Finding the right mental health practitioners to guide you through the process of medication trials, genetic testing (if appropriate), and talk therapy is essential. Treatment plans are *not* one-size-fits-all, and while there is a standard of care, compassion, empathy, and understanding must be the foundation of a good relationship with a mental health provider. If you don't feel comfortable, keep looking and trying until you do. Your long-term success depends on it.

For me, healing my trauma is found in facing the pain, not numbing it, thereby desensitizing the triggers. Teaching my mind to self-regulate can occur when I let an emotion "be" and stay with it for as long as possible. I reach for a "lifeline" if needed and find something positive to focus on. It also helps to explain this choice to a partner, loved one, or friend, especially if they are witness to this process. The wounds can run deep, and the excavation and exposure to them can be frightening for someone else to see. They want to help you, and the best thing they can do is to let you move through the experience. It's vital to communicate this so that they don't experience bewilderment, and effective communication depends on accurate self-awareness.

Despite doing the internal work to combat sadness about my situation, there are still days where sleep deprivation makes me more susceptible. I've struggled with insomnia since childhood, with bouts during adulthood that sometimes last for months at a time. In recent years, the nights I endure two to three hours of sleep a night are frequent, sometimes staying awake all night and feeling compelled to start my day despite the lack of rest. When my mind gets ignited about the past, or financial stress takes over, insomnia comes with a vengeance. Poor sleep quality can easily lead to a depressed state, dwelling on the past, or focusing on bad situations. So, when situations arise that set me back, I take immediate action. If a painful moment comes up, I don't distract myself with any of my usual tricks. Instead, I lean into it by implementing measures that eventually allow me to release it.

For example, if I feel I am beginning a potential downward spiral, I repeat the steps that have served me well during the last few years. I call the sequence RISE because it is easy to remember, and it's the feeling I get after letting go, like a Phoenix rising from the ashes.

The four components of **RISE** are:

> 1. Remember
> 2. Isolate
> 3. Surrender
> 4. Evolve

First, I think about the situation and *Remember* the moment, allowing myself to feel the associated pain. While I am visualizing, I dig deeper and try to *Isolate* the underlying trigger, peeling back layer by layer to get to the root. It's usually less about a current person/situation and more about what was triggered inside me. Not surprisingly, the feeling is usually attached to a past memory. Although something recently caused hurt, the pain was reminiscent of an experience or person that made me feel similarly in my past. Once I realize the root cause, I know I must *Surrender*. I allow myself to name it, question it, be with it, and release it, and sometimes I need to speak to someone—a trusted friend, or a therapist—to work through it. Other times, journaling or praying is enough for me to forgive and truly let it go. Finally, I *Evolve,* making sure I learn the lesson embedded in the pain and experience. I write down or think about at least one positive thing I learned from the experience, or identify a new tool I can use in the future when I will need to engage in a similar self-awareness exercise. This loosens the grip of the past and enables me to move forward, hopefully free from repeating the same response patterns.

The triggers may be different, but the reactions to them express them-selves in much the same way.

With the onset of a trigger, I must get to my tipping point: dealing with and exposing myself to the grief while protecting myself from any destructive habits of the past or making impulsive decisions of any kind. Below, I describe my process, using the intense pain I felt as my birthday approached after my daughter had cut off all contact. I knew that it would entail not being acknowledged by her. Much like Easter and Mother's Day before that, I had no contact, but my birthday has *always* been challenging for me as far back as I can remember. Since I was a child, I never liked birthdays. I wrote them off—dismissed them—by telling myself I didn't like getting older, or reasoning that standing on ceremonial dates was lame. The painful truth was that I could never allow myself to be celebrated. Each birthday reminded me of another wasted year of me being *me*.

That upcoming birthday week loomed with sadness that continued to build as each day passed. By the time the actual date arrived—a Friday—I hadn't slept more than an hour or two each night. I somehow managed to make it through the day at work with a lump in my throat. I left the office at four and went straight home, alone, to deal with what I knew was an avalanche of emotions that had to come out. The intensity of my outpouring was incredible.

Without the usual distractions of shopping, eating, drinking, or venting to anyone, I was left to face *myself*. By 8:00 p.m., I could hardly breathe and was panting from anxiety. My heart was pounding, and waves of crying ranged from trickling tears to wailing. I wanted no one with me, yet I experienced the most intense fear of being alone, like when I was a child.

An odd and overwhelming urge to call my ex-husband came over me because I knew I needed some understanding to make it through the night. He became my lifeline. He took my call, and for a short while, we discussed the unthinkable. I needed him to tell me if *anything* went right and what part he could have played. He did say there was some good, and that was the shred I clung to as the night wore on. Thankfully, he also said he had forgiven me long ago and realized that he could have tried to get me the help I needed. We discussed our daughter; I acknowledged the pain and remorse I felt and said how sorry I was that I couldn't pull myself out of things back then.

Sometimes we need to give ourselves just one small thing to focus on to get through a crisis.

I may have sounded unhinged due to the level of my upset, but I communicated to my ex that I was controlling the situation. I was safe in my bedroom but needed clarity. After speaking with him, I calmed myself down enough to sleep for an hour or two. I spent the next day visiting my son and pushing through the remnants of the pain. I cried on and off, but never near him.

I forced myself to go out to dinner, and some friends joined us later in the night for drinks and laughs (still interspersed with tears). By Sunday, the bulk of the crying subsided, and I pushed myself out again for the day. I learned so much from staying present with the experience instead of forcing it away from me or distracting myself. Although I was exhausted, I felt like I had pushed through a level of grief and gained a bit of acceptance and self-compassion. I allowed my feelings to come up in a safe space with nothing to numb or otherwise mask the trauma. I faced it head-on and named it accordingly. Each time I do this, I strip trauma of its power.

Though it's not nearly as often anymore, triggers rear their heads from time to time and trip my moods, leading to anxiety, insomnia, and sometimes depression. This cycle led me to make terrible choices in earlier years, especially when I wasn't regulating myself with appropriate self-care. I was a sitting duck. That's why awareness of triggers is *vital*. Learning to hit the pause button while you buy time to defuse the situation, remove yourself, and seek professional help is critical. It's also important to take note of any physical changes that may manifest themselves. Over time you will see similar patterns, forewarning you that an event is on its way.

For example, during the week leading up to my birthday, I experienced terrible insomnia, racing thoughts, nose bleeds (internal stress), stomach aches, overly critical responses, wavering bouts of sadness, foggy thinking, over-apologizing for *everything* (feeling inadequate), and the desire to disengage from everyone (isolation). I had experienced them before, and rather than ignore them this time, I made others aware of what I was dealing with. By allowing myself the space needed to grieve and experience the full range of emotions, I came through the experience safely without lashing out at anyone or succumbing to unsettling or impulsive behaviors. After all the years of damaging responses to trauma triggers, this was a huge victory! It allowed me to choose something better.

The best thing to do with negative emotions is to expose and deal with them, question your current belief, and choose to replace it with a new one.

There is power in the inquiry and the words we speak to ourselves and others to describe our situation. But you must desire this change as if your life depends on it, because, in a way, it does. Indeed, your relationship with your adult children only stands to benefit from such a shift in thinking.

Once you acknowledge *and* forgive yourself for what you could have done better, these emotions begin to lose their power. As you come from a place of self-love, people sense your healing, not your suffering. Suffering isn't a badge of honor to wear; it's an anchor that will continue to drag you down. Our healing cannot be dictated by whether we have our adult children in our lives (or not). Even if they choose to walk away from us, we *must* find a way to push past the pain and into acceptance of their choices. The person responsible for choosing to suffer is me. If I continue to focus on the past, ruminate on my wrong-doing, and obsess over my poor decisions, thus villainizing myself, I will perpetuate unfavorable circumstances. I had to choose to change my responses. You can do the same.

CHAPTER 18

Here Comes The Judgment

At this point, you may have formed a judgment about me. You could be comparing yourself to me, thinking you weren't as bad, or perhaps thinking you were worse. I will say that to drive home the harsh reality of trauma, mental illness, and associated conditions, I skipped over the good spots. There *were* some, just not enough of them to offset the harmful parts.

It's easy to overlook the times when my kids were sick and how I cared for them, often bringing them into my big, warm bed for days, keeping bright yellow buckets within my grasp, ice pops nearby, and flat coke to settle their upset tummies. Or pushing the furniture out of the way in our large ranch house so they could safely learn to ride bicycles and skateboards.

There was the time I brought a giant kiddie pool inside during the first snow of the season when my daughter was too sick with a cold to go outside and play. I blew it up and filled it with snow, right in the middle of the kitchen, and she squealed with delight. Or the Halloween she was too sick to trick-or-treat, and cried, staring longingly out the window. Tired and fatigued from her ear infection, I helped her into her costume and carried her to as many houses as possible so she could ring each bell and get some candy. She rested her head on my shoulder as I trudged up and down the long, hilly street. She was not lightweight, and when I paused to catch my breath, she kissed my cheek and said, "Thank you." It was enough to keep me going.

I forgot about all the prayers, warm towels from the dryer post-bath, and the endless whispers of "I love you," even if it meant waking her in the night to apologize for a bad day so that she could sleep knowing I said it. There were endless playdates, reading of books to the point of memorization, countless trips to find her clothing she felt good wearing, and the night I was so proud of finding dress shoes online for her only to realize it was a cross-dressing website! We didn't have Zappos back then, but we did have a good laugh.

Inside my heart, and deep within my soul, I love my children more than anything I have ever loved. In the end, those things may not matter because life is a scale, and the good must outweigh the bad. For the first 30 years of my life, the bad outweighed the good. You are free to judge away, but I invite you to explore what pushing past judgment feels like. It will help as you examine the details and health of *your* relationships, too.

I thought I was not a judgmental person until I learned to see my real self. If you are critical of yourself, you are critical of others. If you see a less desirable trait in another, you possess the same, or you wouldn't recognize it in someone else. We tend to mirror one another for good and bad. Much research has been done on typical biases and how they impact society culturally, personally, and professionally. The sooner we accept the fact that this tendency is alive and well in our decision-making process, the less time and mental energy we need to waste articulating why we are right and someone else is wrong.

I would like to share something that changed the way I perceive judgment. I met a woman who found herself accidentally pregnant when she was very young. Although in a relationship, she decided to not keep the baby and chose to have an abortion. As I listened, I could feel my inner-judge coming out. I had always believed that life begins at conception. I thought about what I would have done if my young daughter found herself pregnant. Would I force her to keep the baby and alter the rest of her life? Even if she adopted the baby out, the memory would last forever. Or would I change my view of abortion for her sake? The answer was that I had no clue. Until such a circumstance arose, how could I possibly know what I would feel?

The woman began to cry, and I assumed it was out of remorse. Then, the unexpected happened. She said she never once doubted it was the right decision for her. She was not ready to become a parent. She was crying because her lack of remorse for her choice made her question the kind of person she was. The lump in my throat became full-on tears. I, too, questioned my inner person, labeling myself a monster for my inability to display better behavior or at least recognize that I needed help.

I moved past the judgment and into compassion for her as another human struggling with inner conflict, just like me. Instead of judging, I *resonated* with her. I may not have had an abortion, but I almost killed a young spirit as I was clearly not ready to be a parent, either. Was raising a child I was ill-equipped to deal with any less selfish a decision? One might argue yes, she is alive and here, but she is reluctant to have her own children for fear they may inherit some screwed-up gene, and she spent the better part of twenty years feeling emotionally confused and unsettled. Who am I to judge? This is the kind of pressure our society exerts on people every day.

To judge another is to dismiss the inner torment a person goes through, irrespective of your belief system.

Perhaps this has helped you to understand me, to empathize with me, or maybe you dislike me more. Whatever you decide, I know in my heart that I have made significant changes, continue to work on myself daily, and live each day with the hope that someday I may offset my earlier negative impact by making a positive impact now.

CHAPTER 19

Freedom Awaits—The Child

If you have read this far, you likely belong to one of two camps: the estranged child or the estranged child's parent. You have different circumstances and needs. I would encourage you to read about the other as a starting point of acceptance and understanding. Having experienced life in both arenas—first as the traumatized child, and then as the trauma-inflicting parent—the encouragement offered here is from my heart.

If you consider yourself an estranged child, let me reinforce to you that healing is always possible. You are doing your best to separate yourself from the toxic environment of your past and take steps to move forward. Chronic stress, trauma, anxiety, lack of certainty, abusive language, careless behaviors, and/or physical or sexual abuse may have been your usual back-drop. Your family and home may have looked good on the outside but felt rotten to the core. It may have made you feel a mix of emotions that you likely still struggle to process today. You can choose to carry on in the same ways or you can choose to break the cycle and pattern. I am not qualified to do or say anything other than to share my own experience as a parent who might have done better, had I known better. Now I know. When we know better, we can do better (thanks, Maya Angelou).

There is NO shame in getting help, sharing your story, and starting to connect the dots of behavior patterns that you need to change. No one should fight this struggle alone. The first step is ACTION. If you do noth-ing, nothing will ever change inside of you. I hope that you choose to find the support you need as a young adult. To not avoid or numb your pain, but to face it bravely. To help yourself and others, finding gratitude, even on your darkest days. There is always one shred of hope to cling to, but it's up to you to find it.

YOU MATTER.
YOU ARE WORTHY.
YOU ARE ENOUGH.

Health, joy, happiness, fulfillment, and forgiveness are within your reach *over time*. Some people believe that no one should feel pressured to forgive and that it is not a vital part of their healing. Because everyone is entitled to their own views on the topic, I won't judge you if you feel that way. It's not easy to think about forgiving people who have hurt us. Conceptually, we may equate forgiveness with condoning what happened, but that does not need to be the case.

When we hold on to the anger, pain, resentment, and lack of forgiveness toward another person, it's like drinking poison ourselves yet expecting <u>*them*</u> *to die.*

You die a little more each day when you hold grief and trauma inside of yourself. Forgiveness does *not* mean forgetting or negating what occurred. Working on forgiveness ultimately benefits you, not your perpetrator. The person who hurt you has little to do with it. When we make an active, deliberate, and conscious choice to forgive, it creates space for peace inside the heart. Some children ultimately choose to allow their parents back into their life, while others choose not to.

There is no one-size-fits-all right or wrong decision. Only you can decide if seeing or contacting a person creates the stimuli and trigger that pulls you backward. A word of caution: if interacting with someone who has hurt you is a trauma trigger, you may *not* be fully healed. It may be wiser to keep your boundaries up and forego such interactions until they cease to be triggering for you or you can find common ground to meet with respect. Working through these situations slowly may yield meaningful outcomes.

I also want to point out that forgiveness does *not* mean you need to get back into a relationship with someone who hurt you. You are allowed to set boundaries that allow you to feel safe and protect your emotional health. Today, more than ever before, there are groups, self-help books, tools, and forums where you can hear similar stories, find support, and get resources to help you learn how to appropriately protect yourself and take the next step in your healing.

To better understand my daughter's choice, I immersed myself in podcasts, groups, and books, where I learned to understand with empathy so I could try to see her life through a different lens. It wasn't her exact lens—there's no way to do that—but close enough. I witnessed the tears, pain, and anger within the stories of adult children who had suffered at the hands of neglectful, abusive, emotionally distant, or unstable parents. I gained insight into how those children learned to move forward, forging healthy and happy lives, and, most importantly, broke the cycle of abuse with their own children. They, too, only grieved the absence of the relationship they wished for—the relationship they felt they should have had. It was a bitter pill to swallow, but it was the dose of truth I needed. Sometimes these stories had a reconciliation; a few even had a happy ending.

Sadly, there were still stories of families separated for decades, grandchildren not knowing grandparents, and the children having acclimated too well without their "potentially still toxic family member" to try again. One woman felt her mother did not deserve a place in her adult life. I felt the sting of my own guilt as I listened to her stoic response to my inquiry about the relationship. "She never bothered to know me then, so I don't need her to know me now." Admittedly, she still felt very emotionally charged when she spoke about her mom. Her ultimate goal was to work through the anger she felt and find a sense of calm when she thought about her mother. She wasn't sure if she could get to that point but was willing to try.

Although I am not a therapist, I can say from my own experience that for me the most real sense of healing occurs when I can be in the presence of a former trigger and experience no ill effect. As mentioned in Chapter 17, Facing Triggers, this is how I *know* I have excavated the deep-rooted pain.

I have spoken with many young-adults, and each had a unique way of handling their situation and finding similar healing. However, most admitted they still felt the trigger response when they thought about their family or parent, so they chose to remain isolated. By the time I came face to face with my demons, my mother was long gone. I spent years after she died feeling like I hated her, but I didn't. I just never had the strength to break away, think my own thoughts, or imagine a life any different from what I was living. I grieved not just her death but also my own waste, haste, and carelessness. I wasn't ready to accept responsibility yet, so I loathed and blamed *her* from afar, often crying, and spending countless hours in the therapist's chair trying to reconcile it all.

One night I dreamt she was holding my face in her hands. It felt so real; I could smell her perfume and hear the shakiness of her voice. "Why do you hate me so much?" was all she said. I woke the next morning, acutely aware that I needed to let it all go. It took quite some time, but eventually I did wholeheartedly forgive her. *All I felt was love.* It was the starting point for me, but I still had so far to go. Even now that the fresh wound of estrangement from my daughter had found me, what good would it do to resent my mother again? It would be as futile as trying to catch all the air in the room with my hands. She loved me with her whole heart and did the best she could with what she knew. I loved her, too.

I invite you to be open, curious, and explore all the resources you can to find peace. A state of peace allows you to be still, not always on the go, engaged, distracted, or surface-level. Check-in with yourself and be truthful. Do you still experience a trigger response? Have you truly been able to forgive (remembering that forgiveness is a gift you give *yourself* so you can move on)? Avoidance alone may not remove or heal the wounds, and sometimes we need to get closer to our past to let it go. Do your future self a favor, and investigate your inner child. It does not mean you have to be a part of your parents' or your child's life, but it does mean you need to reconcile the events inside of yourself.

Time moves on, memories fade, but old wounds can resurface down the line, provoked by the most unexpected things. It's best to make sure they are not buried but excavated and exposed to the light. Only then can one move on in true freedom, filled with compassion toward others and self, and finding a way to look for the good that came of it. It's important to look for the good not because the experience was positive, but because your reaction to it becomes one of purpose, betterment, strength, and thriving.

CHAPTER 20

Freedom Awaits—The Parent

Hopefully, you have come to accept responsibility for your actions. It's a process to finally understand and accept your child's perspective. My early years were spent thinking it was my house, my rules, my way or the highway, much like how I was raised. Well, when "the highway" is an option, sometimes your kids will choose it. The belief system some of us were born or bought into may not have served us well over time, but it can take decades to figure that out. Once we do, the typical reaction is anger at our own parents and a feeling of being victimized.

Eventually, and hopefully, the parent moves out of victim mode and into a position of personal strength. Life happens, people die, jobs are lost, relationships end, and we *must* find the resilience to get back up quickly and not lean on others, especially our children, lest we spin out of control. If our own childhood experience included components of codependent relationships, drama, trauma, fear, lack, or emotional issues that needed attention, it might feel impossible to pull out of the nose-dives we find ourselves in. If we linger in the victim role too long, we develop a dangerous habit of blaming outside influences, or feeling a sense of entitlement for all the things *we* never got, or, worse yet, communicating this distress to our kids.

By nature, children want to please us and often think that much of what we struggle with is their fault. Unable to communicate this to us, they retreat, lash out, and become defiant as a way of being heard. The more authoritarian we become (as a way of exerting control over painful situations), the more they feel stripped of their voices and their own autonomy. Over time, they realize that we will never stop being in need long enough to care about *their* needs. They may move away or distance themselves. They may choose to keep us out of their day-to-day lives as a means of self-protection, and eventually wean themselves completely off the need for the relationship.

If other siblings are in the mix, it can cause an unhealthy dynamic between them, with one picking sides or feeling responsible for the other. They begin to resent their parent's victim mentality and may even lose the ability to sympathize with others, having been far too saturated. This can deprive them of friendships and relationships that need empathy and interpersonal engagement to sustain. The child or children involved, feeling compelled to keep us going, drain their own resources to the point that eventually they turn on us out of need for self-preservation. Sometimes they repeat the behaviors back to us. Neither outcome is the legacy any parent wants.

If you have perpetuated this kind of pattern and your child or children are still a part of your life, you can begin today to repair the interaction. Seek out a therapist, psychiatrist, family coach, or counselor to speak with, find appropriate and helpful support groups to join, and take stock of the behaviors or habits you use to numb yourself from dealing with the issues. Do you hide behind your work, alcohol, drugs, shopping, other relationships, or travel? Step one is to remove all sources of distraction, to be present with the truth, which is not easy.

With the help of a trained professional, the next step is to understand how your child may feel about the way you have shown up. Parenting is not just about putting a roof over their head, paying bills, and giving them material things. It's about developing a relationship. My mother always said, "I am not your friend." And you know what? She wasn't. The parents I see out to dinner with their adult children and grandchildren most definitely incorporated friendship within the parental relationship. They took their egos out of the title and *earned* the right to be beloved. Maintaining a healthy parental boundary by providing guidance and structure is a "yes." But, bullying them with hostile behaviors, mood swings, instability, closed-minded thinking, or uncertainty is a hard "no."

Above all else, when you apologize, do NOT couch it with an excuse like "I didn't know any better." I did this for years because it felt like the truth for me. However, putting such a caveat on your apology diminishes its impact and sincerity. It's not about you; it's about your child. Take responsibility for your actions without any reasoning behind them. "I'm sorry, you deserved better" is a complete sentence.

It took years for me to understand the significance and importance of how I phrased my apologies. This is not to say that we need to beat up on ourselves. It *is* to raise awareness that the younger generation has a different standard and playbook. These children have learned the value of self-care, self-preservation, and self-reliance, and their tolerance for harmful behaviors is much lower than what was accepted in previous generations.

What your child wants to hear is that you own your shit with no qualifiers.

Your child wants to know that you know you were wrong, that they deserved better, and you know you failed to empathize or validate their emotions. They want you to acknowledge that you know how worthy they are of a healthy relationship with themselves. They need you to honor their boundaries, love, and accept them, *regardless* of the outcome for you. This means no "because" statements, just accountability for the actions and experiences of the past.

Once we send out our sincere apologies, affirmations of love, and ask for forgiveness, it is up to them to decide who they will or will not accept into their life. We can change, beg, plead, and pray, but in the end, we cannot control anyone outside of ourselves. Your child may not need or want your apologies, but everyone deserves to be *validated*. If you have the chance to tell your child how heartily sorry you are, do it, even if it seems they may not have a burning desire to hear it.

Bridging the gap between our two generations won't be easy, but it isn't impossible. It starts with us.

If your child is *not* a part of your life, the only thing left to focus on is your own healing. I have a profound level of empathy for those in this situation because it is my situation, too. I know the work you do may seem pointless without your child there to witness your transformation, which is why I urge you to help others along the way. You may initially feel anger, resentment, or outrage. Work through it. There is no room in this situation for *your* hurt or anger. That's what got you here in the first place.

Instead, focus on being accountable for your actions. It doesn't matter if your child was just as angry, distant, or rebellious. This is about healing yourself, and by doing so, you serve your child. The more your kids see your life in a state of repair and not despair (and they will eventually find out, through someone or something), the better they will feel knowing you did not spiral out of control, and are working to change things. They won't own your mess, as they are done with that, but they *may* find some respect for the work you put in after the fact.

I struggled tremendously and won't bullshit you about the grief and remorse I felt. It was completely debilitating. With help, I took the time to uncover my mind's default settings and early developmental issues I did not previously understand. I did this *not* as an excuse, but to help myself to move forward, to develop some compassion toward myself. The mind is a powerful thing. It is powerful enough to have kept me awake for days on end, yet still allow me to function in stressful or demanding situations. That's the kind of power my mind has over my body. In the same way, emotions impact the brain and can be equally strong. They can lower our immune system, send out low vibrations to people around us who detect our weakened state, and wreak havoc on our lives if left unattended.

Your state of mind is the only thing you can change.

You can choose to tap the power of your mind to help you focus on what you *do* have around you, or you can choose to waste energy—spiritually, emotionally, and physically. It's up to you. Claim your authorship and write a new narrative. It's hard work, but worthwhile. It's essential to embrace self-leadership and the fact that, as humans, we are composed of many parts.

When we deny or suppress the more resentful, damaged pieces of ourselves, those dark parts can become the saboteurs within, manifesting at random times without our knowledge. We must incorporate them, understand them, be grateful for them, and love them. It's only through this integration of self that we can become truly whole. Prolonged exposure to our grief, anxiety, fear, resentment, anger, disconnect, depression, or inner wounds of any kind will slowly kill us. *Healing must begin today.*

I have heard it said that people can't change. I disagree. When someone says that to me, I remind them of my journey. When we allow the rough waves and storms of life to smooth our edges, we can emerge like sea glass along the shoreline. What started as broken, sharp, and hazardous becomes translucent, beautiful, and worn for the better. Yet, there is always room for improvement in physical health, thought patterns, and any self-imposed limitations that may still hang on. I will always be a work in progress, as will you. My personality may still be on the excitable, talkative side, but my renewed soul is humbled, seeking now only the opportunity to show love.

The syllabus of life lessons we each must make our way through is as unique as our thumbprints. Within each lesson is a skill or trait so valuable it's like buried treasure. Be open to letting go of, and simultaneously receiving, all you can from the circumstances you face. Pay much less attention to words and labels, your own and others, and more attention to the spaces between them. *Within those empty spaces is where truth resides.* It's not what we say, it's the actions, changes, and efforts after the declaration of our intentions that will demonstrate genuine improvement.

So it is with others in your life, too. Surround yourself with people who understand and celebrate your path, and acknowledge your hard work. No one needs to fight this mental war alone. Your family, your people, your tribe may *not* be the ones who share your DNA, and that's okay. I have made connections with other mothers, friends, and people who are there for me when I need them. Likewise, I will always have their back. These are my "spiritual" brothers and sisters who share in a connectedness that I find hard to articulate.

Once we've done the hard work of accepting and detaching from expectations, the people who choose to see us through a softer lens will be happy to do so. The people who can't or won't do that still have their own work to do, and that's fine. Love them, but learn to live without the need for their approval.

Above all, be kind to the many facets of yourself that emerge through this process. Things may not work out exactly the way <u>you</u> want them to, but they will eventually work out.

CHAPTER 21

Conversations

It is never okay for a parent to subject a child to emotional or physical abuse of any kind, or to be neglectful. It is never ok to steal childhood from a child. Forgiveness and reconciliation do *not* equal condoning the offending behavior. Rather, forgiveness is a means by which we can allow the pent-up emotions to ease, so we can focus our energies on healing our bodies, minds, and spirits. In cases of sexual or other extreme abuse, even intense work in therapy may not bring an abuse survivor to the point of forgiving their perpetrator, which is entirely understandable.

Wherever YOU are in this healing process is okay. I am not advocating a one-size-fits-all approach, but I do want to convey my personal experience and understanding that holding in my anger, pain, resentments, fears, anxieties, and sadness manifested negatively in my body, mind, and life.

If you have been a victim of extreme abuse and *have* found a way to reclaim your identity and control your emotions, you are remarkable. Your struggle can be part of someone else's survival guide. Understandably, you may wish to let sleeping dogs lie and move forward with your life. You have earned it. But, *if* you have the capacity, without the resurgence of your trauma, I encourage you to speak out so others can hear your story, find strength in your courage, and possibly change their lives due to your bravery and vulnerability. You may not be able to change the world, but you can change *one person's* world. Consider that you may become a ring in someone else's ripple.

My journey has led me to meet and connect in meaningful ways with some remarkable people. Some of them were parents facing circumstances similar to mine, bearing similar pain, and ready to try to understand their offended or estranged child's point of view. Others were adult children trying to resolve their conflicting feelings toward their parents. It's as if my focus on writing this book leads me right to them. I can be in a store or a restaurant, or at a party, or in an online community, and no sooner do I mention the estrangement topic than people start to share their stories with me. It's a distressingly common situation, and that concerns me greatly. A few parents figured it out in time, but sadly, most did not and found themselves—perplexed—on the outskirts of their adult child's life. Even more astonishing was the number of young adults I spoke with who were still in contact with their parents and family *but* were precariously close to cutting them off.

The examples they gave and scenarios they shared were so frighteningly close to my own, I saw myself in the parents and I saw my daughter in the children. During our discussions, many adult children would tell me that they really didn't want to cut the parent off but felt they might have to for self-preservation. We shared pieces of our experiences to highlight potential landmines and provide a new lens for them to look through. For enlightenment purposes, I would like to share some excerpts of a few of the conversations I had. Although everyone I spoke with knew I was writing a book and that the topics we discussed would be used, all identifiable information has been changed to protect individual privacy.

"Sarah," a mother of an adult daughter and son:

I used to be so full of rage. Growing up, we had it hard, and I never thought twice about it. We just did what we had to do. My anger was usually directed at things like traffic, but then it spread to work. Someone would say something irritating to me, and I would snap back in defense of myself. I thought this was better than holding everything in, which is how I became so angry in the first place. Eventually, it seeped into my life at home. At times I would freak out, and would say things I couldn't even remember afterward. It got to the point where I knew I had to stop before losing my job or alienating my children.

So, I worked on finding my voice of reason. When things upset me now, I say I can't talk about the situation until I calm down. They respect me for it, and I can step away and compose myself before reacting. I was always so reactionary. If needed, I will take a whole day until I know that my emotions will take a back seat to my mouth. Over time, it's become the best habit I've formed. My kids understand when I say I can't speak. They know I struggle with something bigger than myself. It's uncomfortable for them, and they want to be heard, but they know I will return to them. And when I do, I won't scream, yell, curse, or say things that we will all end up regretting, especially me.

It's taken me ten years to accept myself. I feel like people don't always under-stand when an overly emotional or irrational person says they can't help themselves because we live in a "self-help" world. People think we all have a choice, and in a way, I guess we do. But for someone battling with depression or anger issues, we sometimes can't help ourselves, and we snap.

It was how I was raised, our form of communication. It's been a long road, and I can't say that my childhood is entirely out of my system, but it's close. I just wish I didn't wait this long to let shit go. I'm older now, and I am lucky my kids understand and love me. I could have gotten into therapy much sooner, and we all would have benefited. You can't be afraid of being judged because the reality is, you're being judged anyway. Do you think your co-workers, friends, and family aren't judging you when you are on an emotional rollercoaster every day? Better to find your voice, some tools to communicate your situation to others, and be judged.

"Renee," estranged from her now-adult daughter:

It's unbelievable how I see myself now. My parents loved us, but they were overly strict, and my mother was so critical of me. Nothing I ever did was good enough. The funny thing is, I have friends who grew up in the same kind of environment, yet they became these wonderful mothers. Gentle, understanding, caring. I don't know why I couldn't be the opposite of my mother. I guess I need to finally figure out why. My daughter and I bucked heads from the time she was little. I always said it was my house, my rules, my way. I would really get on her case, and when I look back now, I realize what did it matter? The things she did weren't so terrible.

I had friends who had kids partying, blowing their college educations up, and yet, they took it in stride, calmly and firmly guiding their kids. They would get upset, but they wouldn't act like me. Her father was always the calm and collected one. But I would badger her at every turn. I really don't understand why I couldn't be calmer when dealing with her. Now she won't even speak to me, and everything is that much worse. On top of the anger, I have this depression and sadness. I know it takes two, and there were things we all could have done better, but there is no need for me to fly off the handle the way I do.

"Julie," female in her 40s who struggled with her father:

I was filled with anger and feelings of abandonment as a child. My mother died when I was very young, leaving my father to deal with the grief, confusion, and stress of raising five children. He couldn't relate to us in the capacity we needed. His grief was always at the forefront, and he missed work, lost friends, and my oldest sister felt compelled to step in and be there emotionally. But it wasn't the same.

Before my dad died, we had a decent relationship but I would never say we got close. I always grieved for the lack of what could have been, but after therapy, I like my life and how I feel about my past. I also realize now, much older, that no one can do everything right. He couldn't handle the situation he was in and that was probably the best he could do. It wasn't fair but I needed to let go of my anger so I could finally live my life in peace.

"Karen," a successful, bright young woman struggling to remain a part of her mother's life:

My mother always battled depression and would lash out at us for seemingly no reason. My sister and I were anxious about how frequently our mother would say that we didn't love her. We wanted to find a unique way of proving we did. We spent hours going through old family photo albums, looking for pictures from as far back as possible. The images were group shots, hugs, kisses, and the most meaningful memories we could find. We created a large collage and surprised her with our gift, but her first and only reaction was anger that we had ruined the photos by taking them out of the album!

Karen's story, in particular, moved me the most. During this conversation, I admitted that it would not have been far-fetched for me to react similarly when I was in my unhealthy state of mind. When she asked why, my only answer was that there was something wrong inside her mother's brain, and her anger habit protected her somehow. It was then she shared with me that her mother had been terribly abused as a young girl, and to her knowledge, she had never sought treatment. She said she had never once thought about her mother as being perpetrated against, as a small child, hiding, broken, and full of her own suppressed trauma.

I understood her wound and her love for her mother. She appreciated the validation that she was not alone. I let her know she never deserved any of the rollercoaster emotions she was forced to reconcile in her head. Over the next several months, she worked on forgiving her mother, maintaining appropriate boundaries, and finding that place of peace and acceptance.

CHAPTER 22

Sneaky Truths

One of the most harmful situations is a home where dysfunctional or abusive behavior isn't so terrible that the Division of Youth and Family Services (DYFS) or other authorities get called. Instead, it appears stable, even loving, on the outside. The children are often well-clothed, appear to have everything they want, and their parents are visible in their lives. This "covert abuse" is often overlooked and becomes very confusing for the child because the behavior patterns are not consistent and they're not *all* harmful.

This mixed messaging is damaging as it teaches children to equate love with many negative attributes like I did, and like my daughter did. My push-pull behaviors must have made her feel ashamed, then resentful, then pissed off over her anger, sucked into years of trying to fix things, and ultimately culminating with a final need to figuratively say "fuck off" by disconnecting from my life entirely. What a tragedy. She didn't know how to communicate her feelings, and even if she had, she likely didn't feel safe enough to do so. Worst of all, I probably wouldn't have heard a word she said, given the state of mind I was in.

I hear so many people say, "It's just mothers and daughters." No, it really *isn't*. I know plenty of mothers and daughters who argue, butt heads, and even admit to not liking one another at times, but also generally feel safe, close, trusting, and loving. Too many serious relationship issues between a screwed-up parent and a reactive child are lumped under the umbrella of "that's just the way it is." Love based on respect doesn't hurt. If your relationship hurts either one of you, it may be love, but it's not a healthy version.

It's easy to see abuse and absenteeism when it's in your face, perhaps running rampant with parents who are blatantly struggling with alcohol or public displays of anger, threats, and neglect. It's harder to spot when these behaviors seep into the home environment as a slow drip over time. An explosion here, a slap out of anger there, critical statements at home; meanwhile, hugs and praise while in public. We are covert because our personalities are not *always* in destructive mode. It's the on-again/off-again roller-coaster rides of our ups and downs that cause confusion and distance within our relationships.

In some cases, we need emotional support or medicine; in other instances, we can retrain our brains to calm, self-soothe, and regulate. But the first step, in any case, is *awareness*. Without self-awareness, we continue down our paths of self-destructive, alienating behaviors, ranging from mildly harmful to devastating. We are like children raising children. Our inner child is trapped in an adult body, but the reactions and responses are immature, irresponsible, and self-centered.

Sometimes it's about a power struggle. Parents, who as children never had power, finally come into it from a life of feeling bullied and powerless. They seek to dominate in a strict, authoritarian way, often criticizing or belittling the circumstances their children may be facing. Their children learn this communication style themselves, and it sometimes backfires on the parents as the kids find their voices. This behavior creates a feeling of invalidation in the kids and keeps an atmosphere of tension and anger alive. Although I was guilty of doing this myself, I now cringe when I hear parents speak to children in ways that would never be tolerated in a workplace or school.

Other times it's about the fight. Parents who were raised in an environment of constant fighting see the victory as tied to their sense of self-worth and ability to come out on top. There is no victor in such a scenario; in fact, *everyone loses*. Often, the ego-driven personality must see itself as victorious or superior at any cost.

It can also be about people-pleasing and over-giving. A parent who may have been raised in a subservient way establishes the same hierarchy, just like I did. We seek to please, we overcompensate and play martyr, and then resentment creeps in. Eventually, this resentment manifests as anger. This cycle commonly repeats as we demonstrate a lack of healthy boundaries and self-respect, thus teaching everyone how to treat us. We live in a frenzied state, with cortisol pumping through our body, creating moments we are not proud of. We then retreat into inner isolation, victim mode, and may assume everyone else is the issue, but not *us*.

All these kinds of experiences become a part of the neural network in our brains. We form deep grooves and patterns, as do our children if we treat them the same way we were treated ourselves as kids. This act of misguided self-preservation often drives us to do things that are out of line, and toxic. There isn't anything we really need to protect ourselves from; it's all part of our story, our past. The threats aren't usually real, but the brain sometimes doesn't understand that. I had no realization of the wounds within me. I believe before I became a spouse and then later a parent, the deck was stacked against me. I had nothing to guide me other than what I had seen my own mother do, my reactions almost instinctively mirrored hers. Does this sound familiar? It's a common, almost predictable, yet avoidable occurrence.

So, what's next? Where does a parent or a child go from here?

Pain is not a comfortable place to navigate away from. Sometimes it is much easier to stay in the torment than to find a sustainable path out. The first step is identifying and facing the past and the lessons being hurt offers us. Author and Spiritual Coach Debbie Ford referred to clinging to the past as "staying in our story." It's a challenging but truthful concept. Allow me to explain.

What *does* our story offer us? Remaining angry, upset, victimized, feeling less-than, or clutching at any of the other myriad feelings associated with a painful past serves us by allowing us to have all the excuses we need to not move forward and create healthy, loving relationships. We get to say to ourselves and others, "I can't do this because of _____." We get to avoid the challenge of confronting our pain so we can let go of it. And since we are what we say we are, our story allows us to be right.

Human beings love to be right.

This is where the trifecta of acceptance, forgiveness, and release must come into play. As I mentioned earlier, many people equate accepting and forgiving as condoning. This could not be further from the truth. As we remain host to our negative feelings, we perpetuate more of the same or similar circumstances. I am not making light of this, especially if your trauma was very abusive in nature. That's why seeking help for buried emotions by working with a trained professional is critical, but there inevitably comes a time when therapy brings us only so far, and the rest of the healing journey is up to us. Many people feel that forgiving those who hurt them is as old-school as believing that blood is thicker than water. While I acknowledge that forgiveness is a big ask, I encourage putting the time and work in to make space for at least the *concept* of forgiveness.

I don't condone any abusive behavior, and in the case of a parent/child breakup, you may not be able to reunite. But you can learn to forgive if you choose to. If I can forgive myself and the people in my past who hurt me, I can become less stirred up when I think about them or encounter them. Similarly, if my daughter can genuinely forgive me, being around me might be less emotionally disruptive for her. Like a discharged battery, we emit nothing. Therefore, no one can be hooked by the emotions and energy coming out of us. In Buddhism, this is the precept of letting go of attachment to the outcome. It doesn't mean *you* don't care. It means you can experience and love fully without clinging to what *you* want. I know I have made progress because I can think about the past with far fewer visceral reactions. As for my relationship with my daughter, I still have a ways to go, and I am working on learning to embrace self-love every day.

I don't claim to be a medical professional, but I *am* an expert at confusing the hell out of my kid. It was unintentional, but it was all I knew how to do and I was good at it. In that spirit, let me share some of the less-openly-displayed traits that comprise these subtle forms of abusive behavior. Harsh though it may seem, calling out abuse is a necessary first step to stopping it and healing from it.

Some sneaky truths worth noting:

Covert narcissistic behavior: The word narcissist gets thrown around like a frisbee, yet not all people who demonstrate narcissistic traits are actual narcissists. Although clinical discussion of narcissism is way beyond my area of expertise, I can certainly speak to my own behaviors. I possessed many self-centered, narcissist-like characteristics, and they stemmed from my feelings of anxiety, self-loathing, insecurity, and the need for validation.

This type of parental behavior impacts the lives of children everywhere because children are powerless to challenge it and outsiders generally don't witness it. As a parent, I was often in a state of self-absorption, as any victim is. When we see ourselves as the underdog, it's *always* about us. We are either defending our position, seeking our own comfort, or aligning with the child *after* being put off by our actions. Interspersed are the moments we make our children a priority, causing them to cling to us with hope and experience confusion. Their friends may tell them how "awesome" their parent is, yet they feel otherwise because their experience differs from what their friends see. It creates an unsafe space for the kids to share their feelings with their peers for fear of rejection, negatively impacting childhood friendships. Trust me on this.

Covert criticism: This gem is exceptional. As I grew up, my mother would praise me when I was dressed nicely or had makeup on. It was a habit I picked up from an early age as she wouldn't go out without first "putting on her face." I always found that to be an interesting choice of words. As a result, when I attempted to run errands, see friends, or hang out in my sweats, sans makeup, I was promptly told that I looked like my ugly twin, sloppy, or met with a gaze defying me to leave the house in such a manner. It was years into my marriage before I went out without my hair styled and makeup on.

Similarly, when my weight was under control, I was called beautiful and praised for my shapely figure. When I was chunky and would reach for dessert or a second serving of food, mom would grab the fat around my ass and comment. She wasn't trying to be mean; she just didn't want me to get any heavier. She was always thin and put together, and I felt pressured to be the same. While I may not have done the exact same thing to my daughter, I still found ways to praise what I valued and criticize what I couldn't relate to. Rather than *consistently* giving praise and encouragement when she did things that were important to her, even if they were different from what I would have preferred, I commingled the two. I taught her that "love equals criticism," just like my mom did to me. This ensured both of us would subconsciously continue to draw critical people into our lives as friends, partners, bosses, etc., because it was all we knew.

Covert passive-aggressive behavior: Sarcastic, backhanded compliments were a way of life for me growing up, as was a lack of clear communication, ensuring whatever I did was never done to my mother's satisfaction. I learned to hide my anger, blame other people, make excuses for everything, and pretend to go along with the requests while saying "screw you" in my head. Well, guess what? I became proficient, demonstrating this behavior and inadvertently teaching my daughter how to emulate it as her own survival method. This created countless unnecessary fights, lack of trust, and—when combined with our two sets of rock-hard wills—a mental tug-of-war that exhausted the entire family. In retrospect, her father may have felt he had no other choice but to back away and let us go at it because neither of us would relent. Obviously, as the parent, I should have known when to raise the white flag, but fighting was in my DNA. This combativeness was so ingrained in the fiber of who I was, I didn't see any other possible way of meeting her headstrong personality. I was the "authority," finally, and she was not.

Covert absenteeism: While I *was* a single working parent, with a host of family and work issues on my plate, I could have and should have found a way to be more *present* with my children. Being at home and being present are very different things. I remember watching TV with them while folding laundry when my daughter asked me if I could ever sit and not do something else simultaneously. My response was one of subtle sarcasm, followed by a rationale of how the clothes would get wrinkled if I didn't fold them right away. Now, over twenty years later, I wish I had chosen to have my kids in my lap that night, instead of a laundry basket. *Kids notice.* Of course, I had chores to do, but I let my "to-do" list get in the way of engaging fully. I let "being busy" be my gold standard.

My life ran on auto-pilot most of the time. I worked 40-plus hours per week, cleaned the house most weekends, and thought I was doing the right thing by not enforcing chores. Had I delegated specific tasks, we might have been able to do them together as a family, with the end goal of quality time spent with me being fully engaged. Ironically, when I met their father, he was living on his own. He did his own cooking, cleaning, food shopping, and laundry. Once married, I took all the chores over automatically because I thought that was what I was supposed to do! I had no awareness of my own internal mapping at the time. We were both working, and although his salary was much higher, the reality was that I had a long day, too. Nevertheless, I cooked, cleaned, washed clothes, put the clean laundry away in his drawers, did all the food shopping, and paid the monthly bills. While I felt I was contributing, it didn't address *his* needs or reflect his love language. But it was all I knew to do. Instead of splitting chores equally, I established the hierarchy of me below him, and over time, I became resentful of what I had unwittingly created.

This same kind of "domestic hustle" continued when the children came into the picture. Faced with a family of four, entire weekends were lost with me trying to keep up my ridiculously high standards of cleanliness and order without ever asking for help. By the time I was divorced, I would explode and expect my children to contribute in ways I had never asked them to before. I ignorantly brought on my own demise before they were even born by assuming this overly-domesticated role, with unrealistic and unnecessary expectations and pressures. It killed any chance I had of ever being present with anyone in a real and meaningful way. Your kids won't love you for being a perfectionist. They'll love you for being available, respectful, and kind.

CHAPTER 23

Stayin' Alive—What's In Your Toolkit?

I hope that by reading this story about how I neglected myself by not finding help and keeping us all in a state of uncertainty and pain, you will feel motivated to take an in-depth look at your own circumstances. Not to judge yourself, but to *heal yourself.* To uncover whatever may be running in your background, like a computer program, keeping your thought process shrouded in shame, guilt, remorse, confusion, anger, resentment, pain, or disease, regardless of whether you are the parent or the child.

Why let the casualties of your life choices continue to mount up? The time to break the patterns of the past is now. The time to fearlessly seek out the professional help and support you need is now. Stepping into the power of acceptance, accountability, and recognition of the part we have played in our own lives is both exquisitely painful and abundantly freeing. However, to stand a chance of moving in the right direction, you must focus on collecting the resources and tools you need to make better choices, so you can make the best non-emotional decisions possible and move forward with your life.

The worlds are all connected: physical, spiritual, emotional, and financial. When we overburden our thoughts, wallet, body, or mind, we pay a terrible price. So do the people in our lives.

When I consider that despite making choices that directly blew up segments of my life, I've remained alive, have great credit, earn a respectable income, and maintain a good reputation, it's nothing short of a miracle. Is it brutal sometimes? You bet. Am I out of the woods yet? No, which is likely why my insomnia became such a chronic health crisis for me.

For instance, post-divorce, I'd have been fine if I had remained alone in the townhouse, maintaining my alimony until the real estate market recovered. Perhaps I'd still be living there. With my house worth substantially less than I owed on it, I could have walked away or stopped paying my mortgage. Many people suggested I should do just that. I chose to protect my credit by not foreclosing and using my savings to buy myself out. I analyzed the scenario to death in a futile attempt to find the "right" answer.

LESSON: *Do the best you can, choosing from the options available at the time a decision is required. Then let it go.*

The reason I shared that example is that "Stayin' Alive" will look different for everyone. There is no judgment if you would have chosen to walk away, saved the money, let the bank take over, or opted to deal with a different set of ramifications. *Every* decision creates an outcome, so examine them all and make the best choice from the options you have. Keep in mind that your range of viable options may not be very appealing, especially if your life is in turmoil. You may find yourself trying to determine which is the least bad choice. I finally learned to make a choice, and then to accept and let go of the decision I made. For years previous, I would ruminate, play the scene repeatedly in my head, question everyone I could for their opinion, and then obsessively think about all the possibilities that might have played out. Second-guessing yourself is a good way to shorten your lifespan.

I still work daily on releasing any lingering concerns about the situation I find myself in with my daughter (and other parts of my life). I do this because living in a state of crisis is draining. I had to find a way to change my thoughts so I could go from just surviving to thriving. If you want to make that same shift, you'll need to make similar changes.

Keep in mind that your situation is unique to you: For example, you may not have the financial component mixed into your situation. It may be only the emotional estrangement from one or more people in your life that plagues you. Still, I have found that the people who get mixed up in poor choices in one arena of life usually have similar complications in other areas of their lives, too. Nevertheless, the specifics don't matter. The lessons do.

Life will continue to turn up the heat on the circumstances until we get the lesson.

Although all my emotional and physical losses seem so different, they were all connected by my destructive internal thought process, lack of control over my emotions, and zero discipline over time. Short of losing one of my children to physical death, the emotional end of the relationship was indeed the straw that broke the camel's back—my real wake-up call. Life had been trying to hand me lessons that I refused to learn in their entirety. Now, of course, it's all crystal clear. Everything I thought kicked my ass was absolutely nothing within the broader scope of disappointing, hurting, and losing a close connection with my child.

In addition to therapy, anyone seeking to recover or improve from such an emotional setback needs to fill a personal toolkit. Each person's toolkit needs to be a customized thing because what works for me may not work for you. Still, the end goals are the same: upgrading your state of mind, reprogramming your brain to find and focus on positive things instead of negative, finding the capacity for self-love, and accepting the reality of your situation. Whatever tools you use to get there must feel right to you. My current toolkit has some simple but effective things that help me change my state of mind, which is the outcome I seek.

Day-tripping

The first thing I do is assess, day to day, where I am on my emotional sliding scale, which I affectionately call "day-tripping." I remind myself that I can do anything for one day. Within a given day, I remind myself that I can do anything for at least an hour. If I can hold my urine for 45 minutes after drinking 40 ounces of water for an ultrasound, I can get through an hour of most other challenges. My emotional scale ranges from "crying in my car eating cheese balls while parked in my driveway" kind of bad, to "I did thirty minutes on my bike and then danced around my kitchen while singing" good. In between are days when, after work, I can go out and see friends or crawl up the steps and sink into a hot Epsom salt bath before bed. You get the picture—there are good days and not so good days. Once I establish the kind of day it is, I know which of my tools I need to use to change it or get through it.

Meditation

On the days where I feel I have mental clarity, a few solid hours of sleep, and a sense of purpose, I may only need to do some small things to keep myself emotionally in check. The first of these is upon waking, taking at least fifteen minutes before I even get out of bed to quiet my mind. I would like to say that I meditate, as that's the end goal. For now, being still and aware of the thoughts that randomly flood my mind are real eye-openers for me. My feet have not even hit the floor, and my mind is already trying to pull me into a mental direction that I may not want to go in. No way, not anymore.

I start by taking some deep, long, even breaths. Sometimes I count them if it helps my mind not to think. Typically, people sit upright, but I find lying down and feeling my abdomen rise and fall to be soothing and calming. When a thought comes in, I try not to label it as good or bad and focus instead on my breath. It sounds like a waste of time, right? At first, I would think about all the things I should be doing *instead* of spending time breathing, but after a few days, I realized the time is much better spent acclimating my brain while awake, teaching it to clear itself out at my suggestion. Without proper training, my thoughts run rampant, night and day. Left unchecked, the quieter I am—such as while trying to fall asleep—the more my brain activity ramps up.

I never really grasped how meditation could help because it was always explained in a much more esoteric, probably accurate, way. However, being a pragmatic person, I find it easier to commit to meditating when I think about it as trying to gently control my mind while I am calm. Like a muscle, the more I do it, the more responsive it will become. I want to be able to shut my brain down when I say so, without sleep aids. My goal is thirty minutes, twice a day, and even though I'm not there yet, I keep doing something, working at it. In this way, when I need to control my brain while facing a trigger or feeling overwhelmed, it is already familiar with the process. Brains love a process.

Reframing

Another thing I try to do is to reframe my negative thoughts. People suggest affirmations as a way to tell yourself positive things. I embrace the idea of affirmations, but I find that I have to be in a pretty good state of mind to listen to them, let alone say them to myself. When I am already down, affirmations are not going to cut it. *We won't receive what we don't believe.* Instead, I take a thought and try to tweak it just a bit. It may still sound a bit negative at first, but, after a few iterations of the same, I find that at the very least, it becomes neutral and maybe even leaning toward positive sometimes.

For example, I'd often think, "I will never see my daughter again." Not good when trying to get to work and have a productive, functional day. At that moment, a positive affirmation was meaningless. So, I decided to reframe the sentence: "I may not see my daughter again, but she is healing, and that's all that matters." While this was still sad and didn't stop my tears, it was enough of an improvement from the first sentence to allow me to reiterate it a second time.

"While she heals, I can focus on helping myself and others, so if we do see one another, we will both show up less energetically charged towards each other." This sentence didn't doom me to live without seeing her again, nor did it perpetuate false hope. It was neutral. We may indeed see one another again. If we do, wouldn't it be great if I could manage to not freak her out? In a matter of ten seconds, I settled myself down. This was *better*. Not exactly positive and joyful, but good enough. Sometimes better is enough.

Letter writing

I have found writing letters to be profoundly useful. Since I am a writer, this comes easily to me, but even if you are not, these letters are only for your eyes. No one else will read them. Write a letter to your child, to yourself, your parents, or other family members. I like letter writing rather than asking someone to journal their thoughts because a journal, although helpful, suggests a continuum. It's an ongoing project, a regular thing, and can take on a burdensome quality. A letter, on the other hand, has a finite end. You may find yourself writing multiple letters to the same person, but for some reason, chunking it into a dated format with a salutation and a closing line gives you permission to stop, rather than pressure to continue writing more. I have been known to express total rage as I wrote. Then I'd walk away from it for a day and reread it to see if what I felt still matched the words on the paper. More often than not, I would write the letter again in a softer, gentler tone. Eventually, my anger would dissipate completely and the letter gradually became one of acceptance, and sometimes even forgiveness.

A word on acceptance: Please don't consider accepting something to be a loss or a defeat. Acceptance is no more a defeat than showing forgiveness is condoning behavior. When we forgive, we don't say that the situation was right or that we agree. Acceptance is simply a choice to let go of control. When we accept, we aren't saying that a change can never occur; we are merely acknowledging that any circumstance in someone else's life is out of *our* control. We take the attachment to the way *we* want it out of the equation and stop struggling to change the situation. By doing this, we can eventually find peace within ourselves.

Walk it off

I have often headed out for a long walk, listening to uplifting music through earbuds, while still crying openly for the first fifteen minutes! I've walked by people, and some stare, others smile, while a few must think I'm insane, and that's okay. I know that if I *keep walking* and listening to my music, my state of mind will eventually change. By the time I come home, especially if it's a beautiful, bright day, I feel like an entirely different person. Why? I got physical, and it changed my state. If walking isn't your thing, then take a run, lift weights, swim, or go to the gym. The key is to do something physical so that your body can release happy endorphins. Simultaneously listening to something engaging, such as music or a podcast, distracts your brain from the negative-thought loop.

Find your happy place

Another trick is to associate an area with a "good" day. When I am feeling relaxed and calm, I like to take a bath. I use oils, salts, candles, dim the lights, and listen to a podcast, audiobook, or soothing music, depending on my mood. I enjoy this time and do it regularly. If I come home tired or down and want to interrupt the pattern, it's as simple as taking myself to the place that I associate with "good." As soon as I am submerged in hot water, I change my state as I watch the candle flicker. This is wonderful before bed to let your body unwind from the day. While in this kind of environment, it may be helpful to say positive affirmations or even get an audiobook that will speak them aloud for you to repeat because you are in a better frame of mind to hear and receive them.

Your "happy place" can be the park, out in the yard with the dog, in your living room reading a book, or whatever you find works for you. It should be easily accessible and not predicated on anything that may cause regret later. The simple, soothing association is what you are looking to establish. When my dog was alive, the quickest way to change my state was to sit beside him and just pet and kiss him. The love changed my mood so quickly it was unbelievable.

Note: Depending on how you are predisposed to handle stress, it's easy to unintentionally isolate during challenging times. It's also easy to stay overly active to keep your mind off dealing with the issues. As with most things, finding healthy balance is better. When I find myself beginning to shut myself off from the world outside of work, I force myself to engage. Such engagement doesn't have to be anything crazy, but getting into an environment *not* conducive to a heart-to-heart talk relieves the mind. In other words, get out of your head and into an alternate setting, but try not to talk about the situation. Every moment we spend not talking about the hurt allows healing to emerge. The cure is in there, but if we keep the wound always at the forefront, it will never scab over. There is a time to reflect and a time to rest the mind and heart.

Laughter really is the best medicine

One of my newer habits, especially on a tough day, is to watch a comedy show before bed. I am not much of a television watcher, but laughing shortly before I go to sleep leaves the last imprint and remnants of the day as happy ones, even if for just a little while. Remember, a day is a series of moments. If you can take one moment and make it better, you will find you can also string several nice ones together. The more frequent this practice becomes, the better able you will be to move through the pain and confusion.

Give thanks

The mac-daddy of all is gratitude. For a very long time, I had an off-kilter idea of what gratitude meant. I was always grateful for things like food, water, my home, etc. When I take a hot shower, especially on raw winter nights, I give thanks when I think about people in the world who are dirty and cold. The baseline was there, but the missing link was looking for things to be grateful for outside of my rote thought process. Especially when things were at their shittiest. It's hard. It's like praying for people who hurt you; it sucks at first. You hear yourself saying it, but you don't feel it. That's okay; start doing it anyway. When you are crying, devastated, angry, confused, enraged, hopeless, and forlorn, it's crucial to force yourself to find something small to be grateful for. I had such a hard time with this that I bought a little book of gratitude, and when I was smack in the middle of a fit of anger or despair, I would open that book up to a random page and read the sentence on the paper. It helped.

I mentioned earlier that I would sometimes cry so hard my nose would bleed. Once I committed to being grateful in shitty moments, all I could give thanks for were my tissues during a terrible nosebleed. I had boxes of them everywhere. The mere act of crying while saying (aloud) "Thank you for these tissues" seemed both pathetic and oddly funny at the same time. Regardless, it was effectively disruptive. I had to stop thinking about what I was crying over long enough to say, "Thank you, God, for these tissues." For me, it's God; for you, it could be Universe, Source, or nothing in particular. Once I interrupted the crying and started thinking about how ridiculous it was that all I could show gratitude for was a box of tissues, I began to expand on it. I was wearing a shirt in a dark color. I was able to wash my clothes right away and had a person who cared about me that I could call once I calmed down. You get the idea.

I learned at that moment that I could not feel remorse while giving thanks.

You can't experience two feelings at the same time. This brain hack also holds true for anxious thoughts, fearful thoughts, and negative thoughts. When you disrupt the thinking with gratitude, you experience a pattern interrupt. This isn't a "new age" or woo-woo concept; it's science. It's just the way the brain works. It's easy to not feel grateful, especially when our minds are stuck in a negative feedback loop. We humans tend to lack awareness of the blessings that are in our lives until they aren't there anymore.

To counteract this tendency, try this: each night before you go to bed, write a list of three things you are thankful for. Get a tablet, a notebook, or the back of an overdue bill, and start writing. Hot shower? Write it down. Full belly? Ditto. I know it sounds trite, and you have heard it before, but if you challenge yourself to find three *new things* to write down at the end of each day, over time, you will start to see more and more! The overdue bill may not get paid, but there is always something to be thankful for, even if it's just a box of tissues. There's nothing wrong with starting small.

Mirror, mirror on the wall

Okay, buckle up for this one because it's hard. Also, it's weird, but it works. I am one of those "eye makeup" people. You know, primer, eyeliner, two or three shadow colors, mascara, the whole enchilada. This ritual entails about ten to fifteen minutes of looking into a mirror to avoid poking my eye. I noticed on my darkest days, however, that I would skip this routine, instead putting on just a haphazard coat of mascara before running out the door. Often my hair styling would be nothing more than a bun as well. One day the light bulb went on in my head *and* in the bathroom. I couldn't bear to look myself in the eyes long enough to do my hair and makeup. *Ouch.* I figured if I was that averse to seeing myself, I had better work on fixing it. So, I made myself practice self-care, use makeup, and learned about the importance of mirror work. It was probably one of the most uncomfortable things I have ever done, and—truth be told—it still is, but it's getting better.

Here's what I mean by "mirror work": If you are anything like me, you have a hard time accepting compliments from other people. If someone says they like my shirt, it's hard to reply "thank you" without qualifying how old or inexpensive it is. I also used to be a huge fan of pointing out my own flaws, self-deprecating humor, and deflecting praise of any kind—all huge red flags about insecurity and self-worth. Imagine my reaction to staring intently into my own eyes and beginning to say loving, kind, and positive things. The first five times I tried, I managed no more than a thirty-second glance. I kept working at it anyway. Once I could comfortably stare at myself long enough to utter a complete sentence without the distraction of putting my makeup on, I tried to say, "Bella, you are beautiful." I got the words out but didn't believe them, and that was okay. I committed myself to this practice *and* said "thank you" as a complete sentence if someone complimented me. The first time I told myself, "I love you," I started to cry uncontrollably. I don't think I ever had said something so valuable to myself before.

Start slowly, but keep at it. The more uncomfortable you are with it, the more you need to hear it *from yourself.* Ensure you are alone, free from distractions, and commit to saying at least ten kind and true things to yourself. Like forgiving someone else, this practice sucks at first. It's difficult, but over time it will develop like a muscle. How we feel about ourselves is what we project outwardly. We teach others how to treat us, consciously, or subconsciously. We attract or repel partners, friends, and opportunities with a push-pull force that originates deep inside.

The more trauma or estrangement you have encountered, the harder this will likely be. For a long time, telling myself that I was a good mother was impossible. It is still remarkably challenging. However, I now understand that a part of me was a good mother. I am a good mother now. I would be a better mother if given a chance to try again. Therefore, I need to tap into that inner part of myself. Otherwise, all I will project is sadness and regret about being a bad mother, person, etc. What good will that do me or anyone else who comes into my life?

For the best impact, call yourself by your name before each statement. Say it slowly and meaningfully, and gaze into your own eyes with the love you would show to someone else you care about. Don't judge what you see. Get so focused that you don't see skin, or a face, only the soul residing deep inside your eyes. Notice over time if your eyes seem less dim, or if they have more sparkle or softness. I know this one is really out there, but if you want a fast way of learning where your wounds live, mirror work will show you. This is different than saying affirmations aloud or listening to them while relaxing. Mirror work requires engagement with yourself, which is likely the very thing you have been avoiding for a long time. Below are some mind-altering things you can say to yourself until you mean them and can say them without upset or discomfort. Add your own to the list:

1. I love you
2. I forgive you
3. I am beautiful/handsome
4. I am worthy
5. I am enough
6. I didn't cause it
7. I am smart
8. I am a good friend, daughter, mom, dad, son, brother, sister
9. I matter
10. My body is beautiful
11. My spirit is light
12. I am generous
13. I am kind
14. I am warm-hearted
15. I forgive myself and _____
16. The world needs me

Find your superhero

Seek out someone you admire, respect and trust, and share with them that you are on a personal recovery and healing journey. Ask them if they would be willing to act as a lifeline when you need it, and hold you accountable for your self-work.

I found a good family coach who made a tremendous difference in my life. She cared enough to be gentle, but not so much that she let me slide. Someone too close to you may be biased and not push you to explore your stories, particularly the painful parts. Don't forget to consider following public figures whose work resonates with you. Since we all have different tastes and comfort levels related to books we want to read or people we want to follow, it will take some trial and error to find people worth listening to, but it's worth it. No capes required.

Steeping isn't just for teabags

Forums, groups, podcasts, and books are great tools as well. For instance, for about $15 per month, I joined Audible and downloaded audiobooks that I could listen to while driving, cleaning, doing chores, walking, etc. Some soothe me while I fall asleep, and some kick my ass with eye-opening epiphanies and mindset-shifting truths.

Rather than mindless activities that lead to zoning out, comparing myself to others, or longing for what I lack, I now choose to fill up on activities that challenge me in healthy ways and edify me when needed. The people producing these resources often become my go-to for practical advice. I steep myself in situations that uplift and feel right to me.

Some "self-help" books are better than others, and depending on your style, you may or may not like the books I cherish. What's great about Audible is you can purchase a book, and if you don't like it for any reason, you can swap it out. Easy peasy. I invite you to consider making the switch from mindless to mindful saturation. It's like switching out the French fries for more broccoli on your plate; it may not sound compelling at first, but I believe you will see the benefit over time. It has been a game-changer in my life.

Volunteer

It's true. Surrounding ourselves with people who need our help, who have less opportunity or resources, or who are doing things that bring us joy aids healing on a couple of levels. First, it gets your mind off your own problems. When we intentionally give back to others, we aren't thinking about ourselves. For me, the most beautiful experiences, epiphanies, and breakthroughs come when I immerse myself in talking to someone else about their needs. You can pick up trash from local trails, walk dogs, visit an elderly or lonely neighbor, speak with others facing similar circumstances, make cookies for a local bake sale, food shop, cook for a friend, or volunteer to be a greeter at church—the possibilities are endless.

Volunteering spontaneously can be even better because the anonymity will give you a sense of safety related to showing up. Some days your best will be better than others. I can guarantee that whatever you choose to put your resources into, you will be appreciated just the way you are. No matter what you decide to try, make sure it's something that encourages mindfulness and physical movement and doesn't reinforce poor habits or unhealthy behaviors. The point is to break into new, healthy habits.

Heavy Sigh Here...

It's been almost three years since things "officially" fell apart. I am now 54 and she is 27. Many holidays, birthdays, events, and moments have slipped away unacknowledged and uncelebrated. Things are somewhat better with my son, although he remains extremely sensitive if I bring up the subject of his sister, so I try my hardest not to do that. Like any parent, I am human, and once in a while the urge to know what she is up to overtakes me. When that happens, I will reach out to my kids' father for a quick update on my daughter's well-being. Thankfully, he usually takes my call and lets me know she is doing well and remains healthy. It's enough to keep me going.

About eight months ago, she needed to reach out for something specific to her brother and I found myself talking with her face-to-face. It was hard. I wanted to cry, but I kept my composure. I let her say what she needed to say. I validated her concerns and assured her that I would work with her and her father in the best interest of her brother. I was hoping it could have been the start of a reconciliation, and dreams of sushi dinners and movies filled my head. It didn't work out that way. I was both relieved to have seen her and broken-hearted simultaneously.

We agreed that there is no animosity. It just is what it is. There may not be holidays, sleepovers, manicures, or girl's nights. She explained that she loved me so much for so long when she was younger that she has no capacity to give me those things right now. She hid so much of her anger from me, saved me from myself countless times, played mediator, parent, and valued me above herself. Until she knew better. Once she knew better, she did better for herself. She wanted to know if what she said made sense, and I hardly had the words to articulate just how much it did. I simply said I love her so much that if her moving on from me, to stop the constant reminders of all she mentally carried, is how she will heal and be happy, I get it. I did let her know that I grieve the loss, and she understood that.

We may not have rekindled the relationship, but we *aligned*. I can choose to look at this as the greatest failure of my life or the greatest lesson I have ever learned. Depending on the day, it is a little of both.

I continue to practice self-care, including a focus on letting go of things I cannot control. I don't have my home filled with her pictures anymore; I allow myself to keep just one that I look at occasionally. When I do, I pray.

I pray for her. I pray for me. I pray for all of us grappling with the pain of grieving a relationship even though the person we've lost is still alive. It's not an easy thing for other people to understand. They want to either judge or assuage the guilt, neither of which is helpful.

I remain active in several support groups for estranged parents, sharing my experience in hope that it will help others transition from playing the role of victim to stepping into one of alignment. I encourage them to take a deeper look into their past and the way they were raised, so they are better able to see any potentially broken batons they may have inadvertently passed on to their own kids.

My health has suffered recently, and now my number one goal for the upcoming year is to learn to sleep again, to continue to parent my inner-child, to keep forgiveness toward my mother and family, and to form an even deeper understanding in my heart toward both of my children. It's my chance to parent better now, even from a distance. It's also a chance to help another adult child or parent who may be hurting. There is always a way to pay forward what we have learned. For that, I am grateful.

CHAPTER 24

A Final Word on Self-Love and Authenticity

If you have never read *The Velveteen Rabbit* by Margery Williams, I encourage you to do so. Although it is considered a children's book, it remains one of my favorite stories to this day. Below are a couple of beautiful excerpts from the story, revealing that moment when the Rabbit learned what being "Real" meant.

Being Real hurts sometimes.

But, once you *are* Real, you don't mind the hurt. It isn't about how you are made; it's something you become over time. You can't be ugly, except to people who don't understand. The book is a poignant portrayal of being loved, misunderstanding one's intrinsic value, and the pain of being discarded from the world where you were once so valued.

It's a reminder that we still have value and purpose, and although our lives are not filled with magical fairies, we can endure hardships and know that we are still worthy of love.

"There was once a velveteen rabbit, and in the beginning, he was really splendid. He was fat and bunchy, as a rabbit should be; his coat was spotted brown and white, he had real thread whiskers, and his ears were lined with pink sateen. On Christmas morning, when he sat wedged in the top of the Boy's stocking, with a sprig of holly between his paws, the effect was charming.

"There were other things in the stocking, nuts and oranges and a toy engine, and chocolate almonds and a clockwork mouse, but the Rabbit was quite the best of all. For at least two hours the Boy loved him, and then Aunts and Uncles came to dinner, and there was a great rustling of tissue paper and unwrapping of parcels, and in the excitement of looking at all the new presents the Velveteen Rabbit was forgotten. For a long time, he lived in the toy cupboard or on the nursery floor, and no one thought very much about him. He was naturally shy, and being only made of velveteen, some of the more expensive toys quite snubbed him. The mechanical toys were very superior, and looked down upon everyone else; they were full of modern ideas, and pretended they were real.

"The model boat, who had lived through two seasons and lost most of his paint, caught the tone from them and never missed an opportunity of referring to his rigging in technical terms. The Rabbit could not claim to be a model of anything, for he didn't know that real rabbits existed; he thought they were all stuffed with sawdust like himself, and he understood that sawdust was quite out-of-date and should never be mentioned in modern circles. Even Timothy, the jointed wooden lion, who was made by the disabled soldiers, and should have had broader views, put on airs and pretended he was connected with Government. Between them all the poor little Rabbit was made to feel himself very insignificant and commonplace, and the only person who was kind to him at all was the Skin Horse.

"The Skin Horse had lived longer in the nursery than any of the others. He was so old that his brown coat was bald in patches and showed the seams underneath, and most of the hairs in his tail had been pulled out to string bead necklaces. He was wise, for he had seen a long succession of mechanical toys arrive to boast and swagger, and by-and-by break their mainsprings and pass away, and he knew that they were only toys, and would never turn into anything else. For nursery magic is very strange and wonderful, and only those play-things that are old and wise and experienced like the Skin Horse understand all about it.

"'What is REAL?' asked the Rabbit one day, when they were lying side by side near the nursery fender, before Nana came to tidy the room. 'Does it mean having things that buzz inside you and a stick-out handle?'

"'Real isn't how you are made,' said the Skin Horse. 'It's a thing that happens to you. When a child loves you for a long, long time, not just to play with, but REALLY loves you, then you become Real.'

"'Does it hurt?' asked the Rabbit.

"'Sometimes,' said the Skin Horse, for he was always truthful. 'When you are Real you don't mind being hurt.'

"'Does it happen all at once, like being wound up,' he asked, 'or bit by bit?'

"'It doesn't happen all at once,' said the Skin Horse. 'You become. It takes a long time. That's why it doesn't happen often to people who break easily, or have sharp edges, or who have to be carefully kept. Generally, by the time you are Real, most of your hair has been loved off, and your eyes drop out and you get loose in the joints and very shabby. But these things don't matter at all, because once you are Real you can't be ugly, except to people who don't understand.'

"'I suppose you are real?' said the Rabbit. And then he wished he had not said it, for he thought the Skin Horse might be sensitive. But the Skin Horse only smiled."[1]

The story goes on to tell us that the Boy who loved him gets sick with scarlet fever, and the doctor orders all the toys in the nursery to be destroyed

---

1   Excerpted from *The Velveteen Rabbit*, by Margery Williams, George H. Doran Company, London, 1922.

because of germs. The Rabbit, now old and shabby from years of use and play, finds himself outside in a pile of rubbish, wondering if being Real was meant to end in such a horrible way.

He thinks about the Boy and the life they once shared, and the pain of missing his love becomes so intense that he sheds a real tear. His teardrop, so full of love, makes a magical flower sprout from the ground. It's so lovely that he forgets he is crying. A beautiful fairy appears, and in kindness, reminds him of how loved he once was. She kisses his head, and he turns into a live rabbit. Placing him gently down on the grass, she introduces him to all the other wild rabbits and says, "Run and play, little Rabbit!" The Rabbit lives happily, watching the Boy he loved from afar, who had first helped him to become Real.

The story makes me cry to this day, and reminds me that I was once loved, I am still loved, I am worthy of love, and I have become very Real.

This is me kissing you on the top of your head and placing you gently down in the grass to become Real.

Will you do it for yourself?

Run and play little Rabbit. Run and play...

Afterword

I shared my journey from pain to purpose to show how easy it is to inadvertently pass on broken batons, causing upcoming generations to suffer. I share to raise awareness that it doesn't take living in a literal war zone to create lasting, negative impact or trauma in children's lives. For many years, instead of ensuring that my poor behaviors stopped with me, I unwittingly perpetuated them. Some of you may do the same for reasons you can't fathom. I'm driven to find others like me and share the healing, acceptance, love, and lessons embedded in all my cumulative experiences.

Children will remember parents who did their best despite having little in the way of material things. Sadly, as a mom whose best wasn't even an acceptable norm, I created a nearly identical replica of my own past. The players changed, but the underlying current was remarkably similar. However, this isn't about excuses; regardless of the cause, we don't have the right to pass down detrimental behavior patterns. Unfortunately, I figured things out too late. My mother's epiphany came even later, at the end of her life, when it was too late for her to do anything to change.

For some, signs of the damage and dangers may be present, but they lack awareness of their immediate risks and the brokenness inside. These are the people I pray to find: the parents who still have a chance to fix their shit before the ones they love walk out of their lives, unwilling to try again. There's too little emphasis on what is happening in small doses. A crisis doesn't always begin with a huge bang, something cataclysmic, or eye-catching.

A crisis often manifests in the tiny corners of our minds, in the part of us that we may not be aware of, let alone be able to control.

Some people are naturally predisposed toward gratitude and pleasant dispositions, with a high HQ, or "Happiness Quotient." If you are one of these people, I honor the DNA in you. Many others are on a constant quest to be understood, appreciated, recognized, or find significance in everything they do. This leaves them prone to developing habits like comparison, self-doubt, insecurity, and people-pleasing, as they need almost constant validation. If you recognize these traits in your parents, perhaps you can start to view them through a different, gentler lens. If this strikes a chord with you as a parent, please don't beat yourself up any more than you already have.

Instead, I hope you are inspired to look for the signals you experience *before* you are about to blow up your career, your finances, your relationships, or your life, often for a second or third time! Paying attention to your individual warning signs, tipping points, and triggers helps in learning to manage your emotional responses. There's always an option to think positively, but making the right choice isn't that easy for those predisposed to negativity and emotional volatility. If we analyze the decisions that put us on a totally different path, patterns will emerge (for better or worse) that can allow for some strategic planning and more effective coping.

It may not be your fault, but it IS your responsibility to fix it.

Hopefully, reading this book will help you recognize those inflection points and encourage you to avoid further damage to your life's infrastructure. Despite our shortcomings, the people we are responsible for deserve the best from us, but please also be gentle with yourself. The negative traits and impulses you're challenged by may have been handed down for generations.

Like grooves on a record, this imprint is there, causing a "skip" and repeatedly playing the same thought until we manually move the needle. This kind of thinking occurs automatically, like breathing. We then attempt to regulate and self-soothe, usually seeking solutions outside of ourselves. When that doesn't work, because the issue is on the inside, we experience more frustration, anger, resentment, self-loathing, and self-defeating emotions. We pass on our negative energy to everyone around us and then wonder why the people in our lives respond the way they do. There *will* be setbacks. Old habits die hard, and new wounds creep up, making you want to crawl under a weighted blanket. *It's okay.*

As I mentioned earlier, great writers often begin with the last chapter of their story in mind. They reverse-engineer into the plot via the desired outcome. In this case, my end result is yet to be determined, but I maintain hope. I know that taking myself to the dark places where pain resided and learning to cut the memories free has lightened my soul. Some important relationships are no longer as strong as I hoped they would be. *It's okay.*

There comes a time where one must choose to let go of all the pieces of life, surrender them to something bigger, and accept what settles back into place.

I have a snow globe with a picture of my children in it that I adore. For me, it illustrates the concept of throwing life into the air. Many times during my tearful estrangement and healing process, I lacked understanding of what was taking place. I would shake the globe, watching the swirl of glittery white bits in a flurry, picturing myself inside the glass. For several seconds, I couldn't see my children's faces, but slowly things would start to calm, and bit by bit, I gained clarity. It was a poignant reminder of the process of self-healing and surrender.

As a parent, I struggled with conflicting feelings and destructive patterns, having neither the knowledge nor courage to recognize and fix them. I can now see the red flags that I couldn't see before. They wave, reminding me of the things I used to do to self-soothe, forget, avoid, or create a sense of normalcy.

My childhood home was permeated with strife, anger, and emotional instability. Yet, at the same time, it was full of comfortable surroundings and love; it was a double-edged sword. That's what's so screwed up: amid the chaos and instability that often punctuated my childhood there was also love. As I grew into a teen, I began ditching high school, running with fun and distracting friends, and choosing boyfriends who were more messed up than me. I lived in a world of extremes, battling addictions to food, exercise, vanity, and shopping, and eventually marrying a stable but emotionally unavailable partner, further exacerbating my need for validation.

When you run out of external things to fix you, you eventually turn on yourself. Get the help you need now.

I dealt with mood swings, depression, and anxiety for years, being careful to ensure that everything looked great on the outside despite my inner turmoil. As my self-destructive behavior continued, I marinated in the consequences of my poor judgment and choices. I never understood that once the underlying trauma was triggered, I became a train headed for derailment. Nothing could have stopped me but myself. By the time I learned this truth, my life was in utter disarray.

The fallout from blazing fires, burned bridges, and careless choices took their toll, leaving scattered pieces to scramble after. I have since ditched trying to put them back together again and instead let each one represent a lesson learned and a possible stepping stone on a path forward. It is still a painful journey sometimes, but as I continue along this new path I find I have more love to give, and more hope for better days ahead.

Peace can't be found by changing outward things.

We may desire to shed our circumstances like a snake sheds its skin. There is nothing wrong with evolving if growth manifests gently. Without knowing what is happening within, some of us change things so fast that we uproot our entire lives. Spouses, children, family members, friends, jobs, homes, and finances are tossed to the wind to calm the inner disturbance we feel. It's better to understand why we feel unsettled before making drastic changes we might regret. "What can it be?" is what I have regularly asked myself over the last several years. I used to be super reactionary. As new stimuli hit, I reacted without introspection. The more I responded, the more the intensity of the stimuli increased. It was a self-defeating cycle where there was rarely a good outcome. The same pattern would repeat with the next conflict, and it was exhausting for everyone involved.

Now, I allow the feelings and try to understand the shift that is taking place within. Before acting, I ask myself what could be causing me to feel discomfort. Often, my natural inclination was to blame another person—not me—and this needed to change. Having learned that I can be wrong about this perception, I now push myself to look deeper, drilling down layer by layer, isolating the trigger and past experience. The end result? Usually, it's not the person but the behaviors the person displays that remind me of things I associate with my own pain or discomfort. Suddenly I feel more in control, and while the issue might not resolve immediately, the way I react to it changes.

I reiterate that I am not advocating for anyone to remain in circumstances that endanger their lives or others' lives.

In the absence of that kind of abuse, danger, and mistreatment, I suggest we learn to figure out what is going on inside before making permanent alterations to the landscape of our lives. When decisions are made during emotional upheavals, the reference ranges are wildly off. Our minds, trying to protect us, grossly overreact, create scenarios that aren't realistic, and cause us to retreat into an isolated, self-centered place, like a little child huddled in a corner, frozen by fear. And much like small children, we say and do things that the healthy adult in us would never think to.

The first step to changing this damaging response cycle is to know when to hit pause and remove our hands from the ripcord *before* pulling it. At a minimum, this buys time for mindful exploration and hopefully instills the desire to learn the skills needed to untether fully from triggers of the past. Like toothpaste squeezed from a tube, we can't push them back in once the words and deeds are out. The mess remains, leaving the tube with less inside of it. The people closest to us are, at the very least, subject to the cleanup and negatively impacted by our actions.

I'd like to believe that we can *each* write a better ending to our stories, regardless of the current level of chaos in our lives. After all, we are the authors. The script can change. How can I say this so confidently? Because I am rewriting my own, one page at a time. It is imperative to learn to redefine what victory means and what success looks like. I also now understand that I am responsible for spreading kindness, purpose, and love for the time I have left on Earth, regardless of how brave or fearful I feel.

Bravery lies within all of us, but we must define it for ourselves.

For me, being brave means facing each new day with Grace, despite what my body or mind tries to tell me. My life and everything in it is on loan to me—every person, experience, breath, and dollar. Learning this has shifted the way I cling to things I *think* I need in order to consider myself success-ful, happy, or fruitful. Brave means showing up, exposing your wounds, revealing your heart, and facing your circumstances with the passivity of a leaf in a windstorm. The trees don't get caught up in the swirl of leaves on a windy day. They stay rooted, planted, and firm, knowing that the stark season will pass. New growth will bloom, and although things may never be the same, they will still "be." Although I may not be dancing in the rain yet, I am learning to let the storms of life blow by me. You can learn this, too.

My happiest ending would be to sit beside my two children, laughing and smiling over a delicious meal. Maybe we have others with us; perhaps there is a dog at my feet. The warmth in the atmosphere is generated by the love we share, and there is no thought about tomorrow. There is only the moment at hand. When I close my eyes and picture this scene, my heart swells. Suddenly what I am wearing, driving, doing, spending, saving, or worrying about seems irrelevant. It's the simplest yet most complicated thing to grasp. My entire perspective changed *after* the fact. But you can change yours while you still have time to sit down, face to face, with the ones you love. I realize now that I can't control the outcome. I never really could. However, had I known how to better manage *myself*, the result would have most definitely been different. You can change your future by working on yourself and releasing your past. Today is the first day of the rest of your life. I believe in you. I believe in me, too.

Pain holds a purpose.

We *can* come back from these things with a renewed appreciation of peace. If you have created a life you aren't proud of, begin again, and embrace forgiveness. Nothing can undo our past experiences. However, we can choose to let the feelings we associate with them go. Negative emotions and trapped pain can manifest in debilitating ways. What we resist will persist, so in letting go, we become free.

It is also important to note that while creating physical distance may help to a point, an energetic connection will always remain. Over time, we may find that our hearts soften, people change, and we can become less attached to the circumstances, allowing room for exploration and the possibility of reconciliation, the highest form of love. Reconciliation does *not* mean resuming life as usual, but rather, true healing where *neither* person hurts anymore. We can release someone in love, reconcile our heart's grievance, and yet not be physically close to them.

Prayer has always helped me, especially in my time of need. I used to beg God for a list of things as if I were speaking to some spiritual Santa Claus. Now, I approach it more conversationally, offering myself to be used as a conduit in whatever way is needed. I ask for others to receive peace and healing, and trust that I don't need to know or understand the outcomes I face each day. I only need to accept them. I ask that whatever is supposed to stay remains. Whatever is meant to leave departs, knowing eventually something more soul-inspiring will fill any vacancies I dare allow room for.

There is no "pain competition," no glory in seeing who can best endure the restless, relentless mind, whether it stems from alcohol, drugs, trauma, or stress, or from neurological, hormonal, or chemical imbalance. They are all "equal opportunity wounds." If God isn't your thing, I invite you to call on whatever makes you feel comfortable or enjoy the Toltec or Stoics' writings for a sense of purpose and meaning. You may say, "I believe in nothing," but that's still believing in something. Perhaps, then, you believe in yourself after all?

My call to action? Strive to serve the highest good for everyone involved. Through the practice of understanding, acceptance, forgiveness, and reconciliation, we can get to a place where our wounds are exposed, treated, and healed. The highest good understands that physical distance doesn't negate an energetic connection. When we move in love and compassion, releasing the anger, hurt, and resentment we feel toward ourselves or others, we can learn to be in the presence of our triggers and still feel peace.

This is the Highest Good.

My Love Letters

To my daughter,

I am sorry that I wasn't there in the way you needed me to show up. I was careless, self-centered, weak, and frightened to face the truth and myself. I keep several letters from you in my wallet, beautiful and cherished reminders of you, and I am thankful for the days when your love was a daily part of my life.

You were my first true love and remain so to this day. You were a beautiful child, full of hope, promise, wonder, intelligence, and love. You are all that and more, still. You matter. You are enough. You always were.

I wish you all the happiness the world can manifest for you: pain-free days, peaceful nights, the love of your friends, and special people in your life.

I will never forget the moments that did go well, and when I think about them, I send the love that swells up inside my heart to you. I send you everything good I can find inside of my soul, day by day. I kiss your face in my mind, and I thank God that you have become who you are.

Make this world a beautiful place. Help another person who struggled the way you did. Use your resources always for good and pass on a beautiful baton. Love deeply and laugh often. When you laugh, your nose wrinkles.

Someday it will be my time to go, and I am working hard so that I don't cling and cry for you when that time comes. I hope that I will have grown, evolved, and understood enough to know that in letting go, I will have given you the respect you always deserved. I ask in advance for your forgiveness if I can't make it to that level of growth.

Each day is still hard, but it's more about you and less about me. Your picture still makes me cry, but it makes me smile now, too, and I kiss it every day.

We are separated in the physical, but you will always be inside my heart. Thank you for loving me.

"I'll love you forever, I'll like you for always. As long as I'm living, my baby you'll be." ~ Robert Muncsh

My love forever,

Mom

To my son,

Thank you for always being the peacemaker. I know that must have been so hard on you at times.

You are the one who makes me laugh with your quick wit and funny ways. I adored you the moment I laid eyes on you, and that has never changed.

I appreciate your lighthearted way, the anxieties you hide from me, the honesty you yield, and the integrity upon which you base your choices.

I know I should have done more, been more, shown up better, and never have given you a reason to fear or worry. Despite the many times I failed, you gave me Grace. I am eternally grateful for that.

My wish for you is that you find your True North, that you remain grounded, filled with curiosity, and continue to embrace gentleness. I hope you will always know you are more than enough, worthy of love and respect.

I will always be here for you until I am no more. And even then, I will be with you.

I hope that our journey together can continue and that someday I can contribute as much good to your life as you have done in mine.

All my love forever,

Mom

To my loved ones and friends,

Thank you for being there with me through the highs and the lows.

Thank you for believing in me, often more than I ever believed in myself.

Thank you for thinking of me in ways I cannot fathom: kind, smart, beautiful, loving, worthy.

Thank you for telling me hard truths, even when I wouldn't listen.

Thank you for taking my calls, even when you didn't want to.

Thank you for listening to me, sometimes endlessly.

Thank you for always knowing that I love you all deeply, because I do.

In this lifetime and the next, if one should come, I thank you.

There aren't many of you left, so I will find you.

Thank you for being a part of my journey.

My love forever,

Bella

To the ones who hurt me,

I want to take this time to say thank you.

Thank you for making me stronger.

Thank you for creating in me a resilience I never knew I had inside of myself.

Thank you for showing me a reflection of myself that needed to come out.

I wish you all peace.

I wish you all love.

I wish you all reconciliation.

I wish you all a second chance to do things better.

We all deserve another chance.

Bella

To you my reader, whether you're a child, a parent, or both, you're a beautiful human.

May you find hope in the world, peace in your soul, and the love and forgiveness you deserve.

May you believe in something larger than yourself, yet realize just how big you are.

May you reach the fullest expression of yourself, and teach another to do the same.

May you be filled with a renewed sense of purpose and find a servant's heart.

May you be richly blessed all the days of your life.

YOU MATTER.

With much love and gratitude,

Bella

A Poem for You

One evening as I sat in my bathtub, the following poem came to me. I did my best to text it to myself with slippery fingers as I thought about two people: one who cared enough to slow down, become self-aware, and not take for granted the privilege of serving. The other, moving in haste and thoughtlessness, did not think about the impending harvest.

It flowed from my heart as if I were channeling the words, taking mere moments to manifest. I share it with you now to prompt thought.

If you are younger, you have time to make the necessary adjustments.

If you are older, there is still time, but you may be mid-harvest like me. Take heed, yet take heart, as there is always hope.

The Knowing

The just and the unjust often share the same spoil.
They labor and squander and till the same soil.

Yet the seeds they plant are worlds apart.
Some from the ego and some from the heart.

They wander and ponder, thinking this way and that.
They wonder and blunder as they step up to bat.

They swing and they miss, they fight and they kiss.
Some love, some hate, some search for bliss.

Either careful or clumsy, with cargo rare;
A fork in life's road will bring fruit to bear.

Each waits for the harvest in the season to come,
either joyful or hurt when the gathering's done.

They blink and they think and they choose what to see.
One pained and chained, while the other is free.

The years flash past, awash in a flurry,
of doing and going in haste and in hurry.

Free says to chained "man, why are you here?"
Chained only knows he was never really there.

One sparkles and smiles, youthful and glowing.
One stoops and slumps from the burden of knowing.

Choose wisely, discerning that which you plant.
The reasons and seasons will someday be scant.

Take heed of the pain you may try to withstand,
mistakenly thinking you have the upper hand.

Seek refuge and be mindful of tending your garden
before it blooms and flowers harden.

To know indeed can set us free,
to what extent is ours to see.

Blessing or curse is ours to find
when we see with our hearts or choose to be blind.

~**Bella Ragazza, 2020**

Resources

Although much of this inner work should be done with a skilled therapist's help, you can enhance your healing by steeping yourself in modalities such as prayer, massage, acupuncture, Reiki, meditation, yoga, warm baths, and anything else that feels good to you.

Also, learning as much as you can about the "new normal" you find yourself in is not easy at first but can provide a sense of understanding and acceptance over time. Trial and error to see what feels right and a deep desire to change will bring meaningful results.

I can't guarantee that what worked for me will work for you, because every situation is different. Here is a list of resources that I have found extremely helpful and may be beneficial to you.

Co-Dependents Anonymous: www.CoDA.org
This is a fellowship of men and women whose common purpose is to develop healthy relationships. When you don't know what one looks like, this is an excellent place to start. The website will help you to find meetings near you, and it has helpful information about the patterns and characteristics of co-dependence.

Al-Anon Family Groups: www.al-anon.org
If you or someone in your life struggles with alcohol, these groups help people learn from the experiences of others who have faced similar problems.

There are self-assessment tools on the website and programs specifically designed for teens if you worry that you or your child may be dealing with an alcohol-related issue.

Shay Rowbottom's Heal Tribe: https://www.shayrowbottom.com/healtribe
Shay speaks openly on about her struggle with her family and listening to her content was a turning point in my acceptance of life through my daughter's eyes. Her Heal Tribe is a safe space where people can express themselves in vulnerability and be received right where they are. This group is not specifically for estranged parents, but focuses on all different subject matter and modalities. Shay's wisdom stretches far beyond her years.

Don Miguel Ruiz: www.miguelruiz.com
I have read Ruiz's *The Four Agreements*, *The Fifth Agreement*, and *The Mastery of Love*, all of which profoundly impacted how I continued to show up in my life, despite my pain. He emphasizes "authorship" and understanding that we can always choose to move in love, controlling only our circumstances. I also signed up for his daily reminders, which provided me a phrase to meditate on each day.

***The Body Keeps the Score: Brain, Mind, and Body in the Healing of Trauma* by Bessel Van Der Kolk, M.D.**
This book explores in-depth the many facets of trauma in detail. It explains the mind and brain and their role in developmental issues, including trauma, stress, and abuse of all kinds. With over 16 hours of content on Audible, this was not a light read or listen, but enormously valuable. The depictions of sexual abuse and post-war trauma can be explicit, so caution should be used if you are prone to triggers.

The Dark Side of the Light Chasers by Debbie Ford.

Offering an exploration of how people hide, deny and reject their dark sides or "Shadows" as she puts it, I found this book to be a deep dive into discovering the various dark parts within myself and how to embrace them fully. When we engage and reconcile these estranged parts of ourselves, we can break the behavior patterns that impact us and move closer to wholeness. All that is required is an open mind.

The Answers Are Within You by Debbie Ford.

Ford expands on "the Story," our collection of self-limiting beliefs that often hold us back. When we find the courage to look into our painful stories and embrace them for the positive and the negative, we can achieve freedom. She shares her own story of addiction, and through her narrative and exercises, gets to the core of self-destructive life patterns, shadows, resistance, and limited thinking.

You Can Heal Your Life and Heal Your Body by Louise Hay.

In these two books, Louise Hay—a world-renowned metaphysical teacher—shares her experience of self-healing from terminal illness through the power of thoughts and words. She emphasizes the connection between limiting beliefs and ideas and illness. They are companions to one another. Both books were highly valuable to me as I experienced, and then started to heal, the physical manifestation of my angst and emotional pain.

The Untethered Soul by Michael A. Singer.

A spiritual teacher, Singer explores human identity and shows how consciousness development can enable us to be present as we seek self-realization. He also wrote **The Surrender Experiment**, which was also wildly freeing for me on this journey.

The Seat of the Soul by Gary Zukav.
A scientist's eye meets a philosopher's heart and shows us how infusing life with reverence, compassion, and trust aligns us with meaning and purpose. He sheds light on the definition of "spiritual partnerships" and describes the remarkable journey of the spirit that each of us is on.

The Obstacle is the Way by Ryan Holiday.
Inspired by Stoicism, this book digs into the concepts of knowledge and reason and the importance of staying indifferent to pleasure and pain—an insightful and compelling read.

When Things Fall Apart by Pema Chödrön.
An American Buddhist and teacher, Chödrön beautifully illustrates how to keep living when everything is unraveling. Moving *toward* painful situations rather than away from them can unlock our hearts. Not an easy read, I found myself needing to take this book in bits and pieces. When the student is ready, the teacher does indeed appear.

The Big Leap by Gay Hendricks.
Once you can move past the hurt and accept your "new normal," this book will inspire and enable the reader to identify the hidden fears or associations that keep us out of our "Zone of Genius." Far from just a "business book," Hendricks' straightforward narrative into why we set our upper limits of happiness, success in business and relationships, health, and daily choices was transformational. How can you fix something when you can't identify it? I found this to be a total compliment to all the hard inner-work I had been doing and have gone back through it several times. I wish this book could be mandatory reading for every high-school senior!

The Power of Intention by Dr. Wayne W. Dyer.

I love most of Dr. Dyer's work, and this book was no exception. If you have to start with just one, this encapsulates the belief that Dr. Dyer shared—we are what we think. Learning to manage our thoughts and employ focused intention can be life-changing.

The Work of Byron Katie: www.thework.com

QUESTION EVERYTHING. Through the use of Inquiry, you get to explore the key questions about every painful or negative thought you experience, culminating in the reverse narrative. Every tool is provided for FREE. I urge diving into Katie's videos taking people through "The Work" to gain clarity on how to best apply this tool.

Epigenetics: No "woo-woo" here, as it's been studied and proven scientifically that the expression of DNA can be modified, altering how our cells "read" our genes. There are many TED Talks and books on the subject, and I encourage an open-minded view of how you think about your natural tendencies. This work gets to the core, mapping out ways to change the forward trajectory rather than merely rehashing the past.

Rapid Transformational Therapy (RTT): www.rtt.com

Not your average visit to a counselor's office, this relatively new form of neuroscience-based therapy combines the most beneficial aspects of Hypnotherapy, Psychotherapy, Neuro-Linguistic Programming (NLP), and Cognitive Behavioral Therapy (CBT). Traditional talk therapy was initially helpful to unpack years of sticky memories, but I found it only took me so far. I was willing to give RTT a shot. I recommend it along with at least one traditional therapy session with the same practitioner beforehand to get comfortable and set a firm foundation. I did my homework and found a nearby psychologist who incorporated it into her practice for a few years.

Verilux Happy Light: www.verilux.com

This light is designed to mimic sunlight, and in conjunction with a good sublingual vitamin D supplement, it has been remarkable. I have mentioned my sleep issues and purchased it to help me reset my circadian rhythm over time. Placebo Effect? Maybe. But, for 80 bucks and a 30-day return policy, I was willing to try it. I sit for 15 to 30 minutes in bed first thing (eyes open) while I check my email or LinkedIn. Suggested exposure is 30 minutes to an hour before noon. Verilux has a terrific blog and FAQ section, and will help you understand the benefits of light exposure, which go far beyond sleep. Consult your doctor before use.

***

I hope these resources are helpful, or at least inspire you to dig deeper to find what resonates with you. We all need daily doses of knowledge, understanding, compassion, and wisdom.

You are not alone.

As Tony Robbins says, "Life happens for you, not to you." I hope, in time, you will come to this understanding and find peace.

With love and light,

Bella

ENDNOTES

---

i   Richard P. Conti, "Family Estrangement: Establishing a Prevalence Rate," *Journal of Psychology and Behavioral Science* (December 2015).http://jpbsnet.com/journals/jpbs/Vol_3_No_2_December_2015/4.pdf

ii Dr. Lucy Blake, "Hidden Voices," *Center for Family Research, University of Cambridge* (2015). https://www.standalone.org.uk/wp-content/uploads/2015/12/HiddenVoices.FinalReport.pdf

iii "Negative childhood experiences can set our brains to constantly feel danger and fear." Bessel van der Kolk M.D., author of *The Body Keeps The Score: Brain, Mind, and Body in the Healing of Trauma*, Penguin Books, 2015.

Made in the USA
Middletown, DE
19 August 2021